MW01087631

REALMS OF WONDROUS GIFTS

REALMS
OF WONDROUS
GIFTS

**Psychic, Mediumistic and Miraculous Powers
in the Great Mystical and Wisdom Traditions**

REVISED EDITION

Santoshan (Stephen Wollaston)

With conversations with Glyn Edwards

Independent Publishing Platform

© Santoshan (Stephen Wollaston) 2020

3rd revised edition
ISBN 9781658935630 (paperback) / 9798479503955 (hardback)
A low-cost eBook is available of this edition
Amazon hardback 2021 / paperback 2020

Realms of Wondrous Gifts (1st edition) was first published by
the Gordon Higginson Fellowship in 2008.

All rights reserved. Except for brief quotations in critical articles
or reviews, no part of this book may be reproduced in any manner
without prior written permission from the author.

Design and artwork by Santoshan (Stephen Wollaston)
Printed by Amazon

Back cover, title page and page 74, 88, 114 and 142
photos with copyright:
Text in Hebrew prayer book © Procyk Radek/Shutterstock.com
Muslim woman praying © Opsorman/Shutterstock.com
Seated woman practising yoga meditation © Coka/Shutterstock.com

Contents

Dedication

To spiritual heroes who cross all boundaries and put their wisdom into practice in order to establish peace and unity in the world and encourage a more caring attitude towards the Earth, of which we are a wondrous part.

*   *   *

Reflection

There is a sea of universal spirituality flowing through all the great mystical and wisdom traditions. All we need to do is immerse ourselves into the ocean of this knowledge in order to draw wholesome nourishment from it and awaken to a deep and meaningful loving unity with all.

ABBREVIATIONS USED
BCE Before the Common Era (contemporary term for BC)
CE Common Era (contemporary term for AD)
Cor. Corinthians
Eph. Ephesians
Exod. Exodus
Heb. Hebrews
Josh. Joshua
Kgs. Kings
Lev. Leviticus
Matt. Matthew's Gospel

Preface to Revised Edition

Over ten years have passed since this book was first released. Out of all the books I have written, coauthored or edited it is the one that I have had the most correspondence about, which I am pleased to say has been very positive. One national Christian Spiritualist organisation even placed a totally unrequested free full-page colour advert for the first printed edition in its newsletter.

As originally intended, this book is sold at a modest price. It originally emerged out of a short article that focused primarily on Christian spirituality. The initial idea of writing it was put to me by two people. One of them was my long-time close friend Glyn Edwards, who first thought of approaching me about doing it as he felt there was a need for a book of this kind with an interfaith approach. He also knew me well enough to know that if I did write it, I would look widely and inclusively at the subject and not favour any one tradition over another. I also approached Glyn about being interviewed for the two appendices.

For some, the topic of this book is something that can divide people, get them hot under the collar and quote beliefs to back up their views that are not necessarily accurate. Early modern European history and its witch-hunts show us clearly how ignorant prejudicial beliefs about supernatural powers led to divisions and all kinds of heinous crimes. An acceptance of difference, even today, is not always easy to find in some people's religious beliefs.

Overall, I aimed at presenting the evidence of the research that went into writing the chapters as it revealed itself to me. I felt drawn to uncovering the core of different views about psychic, mediumistic and miraculous powers and the variety of experience there is to be found in many of the world's great mystical and wisdom traditions. Obviously, every writer brings their own thoughts and observations with them. Nonetheless, I have aimed at allowing the teachings and voices of those who had something to say about specific experiences and gifts that are said to manifest on various paths speak for themselves, whether for or against certain practices. In the first and final chapters and in places where the choice of who to draw upon for a contemporary perspective is where my own preference and reflections sometimes come through the loudest.

Like others, I personally feel we can no longer talk about Christianity without considering some of the teachings of what are popularly known as the Gnostic Gospels and have therefore included a few points they raise. Though it has to be said that respected biblical scholars such as Stevan Davies and Elaine Pagels now believe these alternative gospels are not all Gnostic teachings (ideas of a divine light that can be found within oneself and in all life, and a *totally separate* dark creator god) but simply different early perspectives of Christian wisdom that did not become a part of the canonical Gospels. Yet teachings found within the Gospel of Thomas and the Gospel of Mary have since been openly embraced by many progressive and liberal-minded Christians. It is because of the discovery of these ancient lost Gospels and other early treatises and texts that it is now recognised we can no longer speak of early Christianity as *a single unified tradition.*

Coming back to my friend Glyn who I mentioned earlier, it was because of knowing him as a close friend and because he was internationally recognised as one of the UK's finest and most knowledgeable mediums, it seemed like an opportunity not to be missed to include him in this book, particularly as he was once a Benedictine monk at a famous monastery, studied the lives and teachings of many of the great masters of spirituality and had his own insightful perspectives to share about various powers and gifts that can unfold. It was for this reason that I included the two interviews with him, in which he eloquently answered some difficult questions and shared thoughts I had not heard him talk about before. Within the reflections he shared, it is easy to detect teachings and wisdom about our collective responsibility for each other and our sacred Earth. For ultimately, we are all a part of a single family, eternally evolving in the one interrelated Spirit that seeks harmonious expression in and through all. In our multi-faith world, I can only hope those who do not come from the same background as Glyn will nonetheless find what he had to share from a lifetime of experience and knowledge, of beneficial interest.

In addition, a glossary of terms linking with different areas that are looked at in this book has also been included. It was not something I was thinking of including, but a couple of people who looked over early drafts of the first edition felt it would be beneficial to have.

Readers will notice that this book does not focus on arguments about whether some accounts such as popular legends about key individuals of the East and West or miraculous happenings in the Christian and Hebrew Bible should be considered as factual or not. For it is moving into the realms of personal belief and is the topic for another type of book and those who feel drawn to picking over the bones of historical and scriptural inaccuracies, contradictions and controversies, such as Bart D Ehrman and his fascinating studies and books, including *Jesus, Interrupted: Revealing the Hidden Contradictions in the Bible* – although I have offered alternative perspectives about matters for consideration in various places.

*   *   *

Acknowledgements

I wish to thank Glyn Edwards and Graham Hewitt for approaching me with the idea of writing this book and for encouraging me to expand upon a piece I had written for the book *The House of Wisdom: Yoga Spirituality of the East and West*. A special thanks also goes to Mantra Books for allowing extracts of the original piece to be used.

*   *   *

Introduction

There was a time when writing a book of this kind would have been considered as being out of touch with current thinking by the scientifically minded – although it is still sadly the case that there are many who insist on hanging onto a split between spirituality and science. The hypothesis put forward by James Frazer in *The Golden Bough*, published over a hundred years ago, was that humans have evolved from mythical indigenous beliefs in magic and in many spirits interrelated with nature and tribal communities who respected the Earth's biodiversity, to formalised religions influencing the structures of the great civilisations of history, to a scientific age and way of relating to life and the Universe that has no need for the beliefs and practices of the previous two stages.

For some, Frazer's path to cold scientific and dualistic logic holds the final view, and for many years mechanistic science was thought to have proven once and for all that life was nothing mysterious and promoted ideas about nature needing to be controlled, dominated and paid little respect. A spirit world or a sacred Earth to be celebrated, revered, cherished and lived in harmony with, or a Cosmos with spiritual implications and purpose, were pushed aside in favour of theories about life and the planets being nothing more than regulated machines with no creative mind permeating and underlying them, and no room for such things as psychic, shamanistic and mediumistic phenomena, the miraculous, or ideas about the sacredness of existence.

Yet this is not the end of the story. For we currently live in exciting times, where some physicists and scientific philosophers such as Joel Primack and Nancy Ellen Abrams are discovering that humans hold a special place in a living Universe that is not without significance. Some contemporary scientists are validating psychic phenomena and transcendent and spiritual realms of experience as fact and have once again joined the search to discover what they imply and how we can best understand and awaken to diverse powers related to life – seeking how to responsibly manifest different abilities and live in harmony with the realms of nature and spirituality with which they connect.

Similar to Carl Jung's theory about the Collective Unconscious, the studies and theory of the Cambridge biologist Rupert Sheldrake into Morphogenetic Fields and Resonance (a biological field permeating nature that contains information to shape the exact form of living things as well as behaviour) point to an interconnected creative and psychic mind of the world and all life. In John David Ebert's *Twilight of the Clockwork Gods* he mentions how doctors such as Richard Gerber, Larry Dossey and Deepak Chopra are taking ancient microcosomologies seriously, as well as Yogic beliefs about *kundalini* and *pranic* energy. A spirit world, a sacred Earth, telepathy, angels, reincarnation and the existence of the soul are all areas for earnest discussion for various respected contemporary scientists and doctors.

Ebert mentions how the Princeton Engineering Anomalies Research Program have meticulously documented the reality of paranormal phenomena such as telepathy, psychokinesis and remote viewing. In the DVD version of the excellent *What the Bleep do We Know?* (extended English version) Dr Dean Radin, a senior scientist at the Institute of Noetic Sciences, mentions how it is no longer a case of asking whether scientists believe in psychic abilities or not as many of them do. Contemporary terms such as 'precognitive events' are now being employed by them to investigate an array of spiritual, mediumistic and psychic phenomena and wisdom.

With this in mind, let us look at some traditional myths, accounts and documented comments and experiences of various yogis, mystics, seers and prophets and their teachings about them and search for a central core that might unite them. But before we do this, I feel it is wise to reflect on some areas that connect with the subject, which are explored in the following chapter.

*   *   *

1
Ancient Wisdom, Postmodern World

There are different kinds of spiritual gifts,
but they all come from the same Spirit.
~ CORINTHIANS 12:4

What are often classified as supernormal powers can be seen to connect with various forces of nature, such as having control over the weather or other natural phenomena. They can also be seen to connect with prophecies about coming events, communicating with angels and spirits, numerous states and stages of meditation, ultimate levels of spiritual being and various types of healing. The word miracle refers to an event that is invariably attributed to have happened through the intervention of a divine being or a higher spiritual force, and because of this, miracles are generally looked upon as beyond ordinary scientific explanation and not bound by nature's laws.

Over the last hundred years, there has been a blurring of different types of spiritual, mediumistic and psychic experience. While it can at times be difficult to draw a clear

REALMS OF WONDROUS GIFTS

line between where one type of experience ends and another begins, it is a mistake to reduce everything to a single category. One cap cannot be made to fit all.

Some years ago, I came across an extensive booklet entitled *Psychic Influences in World Religion*, written with deep conviction by the Spiritualist James F Malcolm and noticed he attempted to place a variety of experiences, including mystical ones, under headings of such things as spirit contact and mediumship. But if we look at what the word mediumship implies, we see that it generally refers to an ability to see, hear or feel spirit personalities that no longer have physical existence. Additionally, physical and trance mediumship and healers who are said to be aided by spirit personalities are other areas that can fall under this heading.

The word mediumship literally refers to someone who is seen to be in the middle of two realms of existence – the physical world and the spirit world – and acts as a mediator between them. These two realms of experience that are often mentioned by mediums and shamans can be seen as quite different from the understanding of oneness/non-separateness, and unity that is realised by many of the great mystics, where everything shares an interconnected underlying divinity.

Those following mystical paths invariably focus on a life of the heart (historically there have been intellectual, philosophical paths of mysticism as well, such as the Sober School in Sufism), prayer and/or meditation, reflection, work and spiritual discipline, and dedicate themselves to serving and discovering unity with the divine, which is found in all activities of life, yet also transcends all and in which all things possess an interactive relationship. While some mystics appear to display mediumistic types of experience and phenomena, Swami Abhayananda's enlightenment experience, which occurred in 1966, shows us that some do not and demonstrates how simply calling a mystic a medium is misleading:

> *I was not privy to the so-called 'subtle' realms of spirit; I saw nothing there of angels, spirit-guides, or souls. This does not imply that these do not exist ... My vision was one of identity with the Eternal, my original transcendent Source and ultimate being. I was able to see ... the outflux and influx of the universal cosmos.*

A Blossoming of Extraordinary Gifts

When we look at the beginnings of a religion we frequently find there are reports of such things as profound meditational experiences, or we find a founder or an early leader displaying supernormal gifts. In the course of a religion's history we invariably find holy men and women displaying various powers such as healing and prophecy. Ancient scripture such as the Old and New Testament, the Yoga Sutra and the Bhagavata Purana mention a variety of phenomena that include the hearing of divine voices, visions, reading other people's minds and levitation. We hear about contemporary charismatic Christians speaking in tongues, technically termed 'glossolalia', and various mystics performing extraordinary feats. Tibetan Buddhists have long made use of oracles, who are said to go into trance states and become possessed by various deities.

One might argue that such things as oracles are nothing to do with spirituality. But if spirituality is seen as a way of life and discipline and oracles are being consulted as guides about various aspects of it, then they are obviously a part of it in some way. However, although this overview of five of the world's great mystical and wisdom traditions shows that certain types of psychic, mediumistic and miraculous powers can be found and practised within them, there is a general belief in not placing *too much* emphasis on them, which often comes through clearly as something that needs to be considered. For we must never look upon the parts as being greater than the whole.

Problems with Miracles

With the subject of miracles there are ethical dilemmas and teachings that contradict the need for the display of any supernatural powers. We are told in various teachings that if we wish to find a lasting peace we must at first accept things as they are. There is indeed great wisdom to this. Yet if we passively accept all things as they truly are, then the need for a miracle to occur to change anything would not arise. In addition to this, people who have disabilities sometimes tell us they are not looking for a miracle that makes them the same as everyone else but would rather people simply accepted them the way they are.

A positive change might be desired because of an inability to include all life. We therefore have to be careful that we are not using spirituality and various practices as a form of avoidance. We may also notice a tendency at times to want to jump in and quickly fix various difficulties people face, which can display this inability to embrace negative aspects of life. In a recent TED Talk, psychologist Susan David spoke about negativity becoming a new taboo and how discomfort is in fact the price we pay for a meaningful life. We of course need to endeavour to be there for others in a supportive role and exhibit spontaneous and natural acts of compassion, but a quick-fix remedy is not always an authentic display of empathy with others.

There are also problems when it comes to miracles not happening, as it could be interpreted that people's prayers are not being answered or that their practices are ineffective, or even that they are meant to suffer in some way, which would seem like a harsh and inhumane position to take. However, many miracles, if we wish to call them this, can be seen as not so much about changing physical circumstances but bringing about a proactive acceptance of a situation. This kind of miracle does not physically favour people over others who might be less fortunate than them. An example of this is when suffering brings about a wholesome transformation in people's lives that awakens them to connecting more positively with life and others.

Suffering can at times open the doors to profound spiritual and mystical experiences that help to bring about new and healthier states of being. But as we know, this does not always happen, and there are no satisfactory answers as to why some people have these experiences in dark hours of need while others do not.

When it comes to healing we have to consider the

findings of medical science that inform us there are illnesses, even terminal ones, from which people can go into remission. Additionally, there is also the placebo effect to bear in mind. None of this undermines the infinite possibilities of healing but leads us to realise there is much we still do not know about the power of the mind and the body's ability to heal itself.

Synchronicity

Some scholars have looked for rational and scientific explanations for some of the Bible's miracles, such as what natural event might have caused the Red Sea to dry up just as Moses and the Israelites needed to cross it (Exod. 14:21-22) or could have changed the water of the Nile to the colour of blood, kill fish that lived in it and made it undrinkable (Exod. 7:17-18). Even if natural explanations are found for such phenomena, it is the way that the events are seen to happen at a specific time that gives them greater significance. Synchronistic events can therefore be seen as miraculous happenings. Drawing on Carl Jung's theory about them, some people have come to consider synchronistic events as having deep spiritual meaning as illustrated in James Redfield's popular fictional book and film *The Celestine Prophecy*.

Problems with Experiences

Within all beliefs there are followers who want to claim the experiences and phenomena that unfold in their tradition show that their path holds the final truth or that they have been chosen over others as special in some way. Some go as far to condemn anyone displaying supernatural powers or having deep spiritual experiences outside of their tradition as false. Or even worse, that they are being misled by demonic forces!

In Carl Jung's autobiography, he reminds us that concepts are often built around experiences that can lose much of what they are about. Deepak Chopra tells us that, 'Finding the truth is not a matter of making anyone wrong, but of seeing how every belief can be expanded'. But no matter what experiences are encountered on spiritual journeys, they need to lead to an opening to the transforming influence of the divine that is within, transcends and unites all.

In today's world we can take routes that do not rely on religious dogmas of the past but can still fall into familiar traps, as we might believe our experiences or practices give us the ultimate perspective on spirituality, the spirit world or life after death. Problems arise when the whole of development is overlooked in place of only one or two facets such as only considering the philosophical and theological aspects of a belief system, or just the traditional realms of mystical and psychic experiences. The mind and heart need to work *together*. Though in the ultimate sense, all things become parts of mystical experience when the spiritual life is lived to its full and absolute profoundest level of understanding.

An integral and holistic approach implies bringing *all parts* together in order to discover a balance and harmony with the many facets of life. For the majority of the great mystics, lamas and yogis, study, the development of the mind, everyday life, work and practices of prayer and meditation are unifying facets of the whole of spirituality. It is not a life of escapism and blissing out but spiritually living and acting in the world and using all our powers for good.

Deeper Mysteries

When thinking about the views some have against psychic, shamanistic, mediumistic and so-called miraculous powers, one question that keeps coming to mind is, 'Doesn't wholeness and oneness include everything?' After all, the New Testament tells us that God is in all (Eph. 4:6).

Obviously, there are more subtle dimensions to consider in the great wisdom and mystical traditions than simply wholeness and oneness. However, they are indispensable central elements that profoundly link with them. For instance, the Sanskrit word 'yoga' comes from the verbal root *yuj*, meaning 'to yoke/bind together' and is often interpreted as unity with the divine. In a talk given at the Christian Meditation Centre in London by the highly respected Benedictine monk Father Lawrence Freeman, he described the word 'holiness' as being a comparable word to 'wholeness'. In the Bible, holiness is about overcoming separateness from the divine. So it seems that both words, 'yoga and holiness', imply something very similar, if not identical, which suggests an inclusion and integration of the many facets of our being with the divine that exist in all.

Further to this, the mystical strands running through various traditions invariably include realms of unitive consciousness experienced when we are fully present with all things, which overcome restrictions of separate individual awareness: our limited sense of self.

In the Buddha's teachings, though we cannot technically talk about them as mystical (as a mystic is someone who follows a path grounded in the divinity of God, which the Buddha did not teach), we find mention of an ultimate state of non-separateness. We can, therefore, conclude that many of the great wisdom and mystical traditions appear to share similarities in the different terms they use. And if all life is interconnected and is a part of a greater whole, it then must follow that such things as psychic, mediumistic and miraculous powers are facets of this interwoven reality. It would be odd to leave something out and call it 'whole' otherwise. Although from a supreme perspective some may teach about a transcendence of all things, this transcendence, if looked at in a healthy and practical way, need not imply denying any parts. It can be about *including* and *transcending*, as the Integral philosopher Ken Wilber informs us.

However, there is one area that does not fit so neatly with this view, as there are various extreme ascetics in many traditions who have renounced the world and normal contact with it, which is hardly about inclusiveness though accounts of such people often mention them possessing and displaying a variety of supernatural powers. But it should be mentioned that completely renouncing the world is rarely practised or even favoured in many traditions. It was not the path of the first guru of the Sikh faith (Guru Nanak), the Buddha (although he tried harsh ascetic practices at first, he found they did not lead to enlightenment), Moses, the Prophet Muhammad or Jesus, who went into the desert for 40 days but then went back into society. The central message of one of Hinduism's most revered holy books, the Bhagavad Gita, is about involvement in the world rather than escaping from it and puts forward a belief in extreme world-renouncing practices not achieving their aim.

Problems with Language

In writing about such a vast topic as psychic, mediumistic and miraculous powers in some of the world's great wisdom and mystical traditions, it soon becomes clear there are problems with terminology and the way these powers are considered. For what might be classed as an extrasensory faculty by some might be seen as a miraculous gift by others.

We also need to take into consideration that any practice such as prayer or meditation which is believed to have a result or effect in some way, is basically a belief in psychic or miraculous power. Even if there is a psychological or physiological explanation for what happens such as feeling more relaxed after calming one's breath. If an individual holds a belief in a power that brings about a transformation, it implies a belief in a psychic or miraculous force that can interact with his or her life and bring about positive changes. When bread is consecrated by a Roman Catholic priest during Mass and is believed to transform into the body of Christ, it obviously implies a belief in a miraculous power.

To complicate matters further, we could consider as Carl Jung did that we can know nothing of life if it were not for our psychic senses, as everything can be seen as being perceived by and processed through them. For ultimately, we experience everything as a psychic image in one way or another, i.e. in symbolic form, which has symbolic meaning for us, including language and all other sensory data. Visualisation practices can for instance be viewed as a way of entering into and working with the deeper psychic levels of our being.

Whatever conclusion we wish to make, it is clear that teachings about and people's experiences of psychic or miraculous gifts, although some might argue are not essential to spiritual and mystical life are, as will be seen in the examples given in this book, intrinsically bound up with and frequently by-products of it. It is only when we do not heed the general warning given about overattachment to such things and allow them to distract us from other realms of development and use them purely for self-promotion that they become obstacles to spiritual living. For the path is multifaceted and everyone is uniquely different with an infinite variety of gifts to share, which does not imply an I am more important than anyone else egocentricness:

> *[L]et your light shine before others, so they may see your good works and give glory to your Father [/Mother-God] in heaven.*
> ~ MATTHEW'S GOSPEL 5:16

Familiar and Contemporary Beliefs

As mentioned, there are some that claim such things as mediumship and shamanism should not be practised. Popular passages for such believers are found in the Old Testament, particularly sections of Deuteronomy. Yet even Jesus is reported to have consulted with the departed spirits of Moses and Elijah (Matt. 17:3 and Luke 9:30). Deuteronomy fails to mention that psychic and mediumistic types of abilities have been known to surface naturally within people's spiritual growth, even when they have not consciously been trying to develop them, as fellow author of *The House of Wisdom*, Swami Dharmananda Saraswati, discovered to her surprise when undertaking various yoga practices, or what people are meant to do if this happens.

The reason for one of the warnings given in Deuteronomy is because it will make us ritually unclean if we associate with certain people (19:31). This goes against any wholesome ideas of a spiritual inclusiveness and contrasts strongly with other passages in the Old Testament that remind us to 'love our neighbour as our self' (Lev. 19:18), which the Jewish people are called to live and Jesus advocated as the second greatest commandment after loving God with all one's heart, mind and soul (Matt. 22:37-39). The combining of these two teachings has been called 'the Jesus Creed' by some Christians such as Scot McKnight, which amends the ancient Jewish *Shema*/prayer: 'Hear, O Israel: the Lord is our God, the Lord alone' (a popular alternative to the last three words is 'the Lord is one').

Other warnings in Deuteronomy are about divination, sorcery and witchcraft (18:10-12), of which the latter has links to various cultures with Paganistic beliefs that are often about honouring the Divine Feminine and being at one with nature and the Earth, which in today's world are especially important practices, particularly because of climate change and the harm us humans are inflicting on other species and the environment. Ignoring a Gaia-centred spirituality has been looked upon as a serious mistake by many contemporary pioneers of nature-centred spirituality such as Matthew Fox and the late Thomas Berry, and has been seen as a contributory factor that has caused humankind to not care enough about other species and the future of Earth-life.

The medium that Saul is described visiting in the Old Testament's First Book of Samuel, who makes contact with the deceased spirit of Samuel, reminds him how he had expelled people such as her from the land, which shows a harsh form of persecution that would be unacceptable to any human rights believer.

On the whole, fundamentalist strands of any tradition will want to read holy scripture as a word for word factual document that needs little or no interpretation. Yet there is a problem with this approach, as there are invariably contradictory and ambiguous teachings in all the world's great wisdom and mystical traditions and scriptures, as well as plenty of symbolic and metaphorical language used and perspectives on life that are no longer valid. This means that all teachings require personal reflection to arrive at one's own understanding and insights in order to make sense of them. The cultivation of wisdom and personal reflection are highly prized in all healthy spiritual practices, whereas fundamentalist beliefs, on the other hand, rely on having all the answers and discourage any individual exploration that goes beyond set perimeters. Jewish mystic, healer and psychotherapist Estelle Frankel pithily warns us that, 'In matters of faith, in particular, too much certainty can shut down the process of spiritual inquiry'.

We need to remember that one person's truth can mean little to someone from another faith and that ancient teachings were given in times that were different from the world in which we live. (Even 30 year old studies on psychic, mediumistic and miraculous powers in world religions will be out of touch with contemporary thinking.) Hopefully, we would not put someone to death for working on the Sabbath (Exod. 35:2), as it is not only barbaric but fails to see that every day is holy and how having a vocation is a part of spiritual life. Teachings from other eras and traditions remind us that good works and wholesome and skilful actions are essential for balanced living.

The societies in which the historical Buddha, the first prophets and many of the early mystics grew up in cannot be compared completely with ours. The world in which we live is even vastly different from the one our parents grew up in when they were our age, and our understanding of science, spirituality, religion and the Universe has changed. Having an I am right and you are wrong intolerance will only create problems in our pluralistic, contemporary multicultural and multi-faith world.

Changes in Thinking and Understanding

Many contemporary scientists and influential thinkers are bringing about changes in our understanding of the various powers we possess and how they relate to underlying forces at work throughout the Universe. Some scientists, for example, are discovering things that were once looked upon as supernatural, such as precognition, as being perfectly natural phenomena that connect us with all life as they are bound up with an interactive creative consciousness underlying everything (see pages 16 to 17). In contrast to this, we find some attitudes of 40 years ago were not so open. Although taking an opposite view himself, Frits Staal pointed out in his excellent book *Exploring Mysticism*, published in 1975, that, 'In modern scholarly literature such powers are frowned upon, and it is generally suggested that Patanjali [the compiler of the influential Yoga Sutra] himself also looked down on them'.

Even in early Buddhism, the beginning of section 11 of the Kevavaddha Sutta of the Digha Nikaya mentions the exercise of supernormal powers, in which the Buddha condemns as vulgar conjuring tricks. According to the relatively recent *Rider Encyclopedia of Eastern Philosophy*, all the great masters have cautioned against psychic and miraculous powers because they 'belong entirely to the phenomenal realm and contribute nothing to one's realisation of absolute truth, and because attachment to such abilities constitutes a serious obstacle in the way to spiritual development'.

Various yogis, such as the 20th century teacher Gopi Krishna, warned against using miraculous powers and stated that, 'Not one of the great modern Indian saints and sages such as Sri Ramakrishna, Maharshi Ramana, Sri Aurobindo, Swami Dayananda, or Swami Sivananda, endorsed the exhibition of psychic gifts or the working of miracles, even if endowed with such powers'.

Yet we find Aurobindo writing extensively about our psychic being and experiences attainable in dreams and meditation. He even experimented with automatic writing after his brother introduced him to it and produced various amounts of teachings through the practice, where what appeared to be a discarnate spirit personality wrote about different spiritual topics. Aurobindo even produced the short book *Yoga Sadhana* by the method, at the rate of one chapter a day and completed it in roughly seven to eight days. Interestingly in Volume Two of his published diaries, he came to the conclusion that the writings were 'not always of a higher order', and according to his experience he felt that the majority but not all 'of such writings comes from a dramatising element of the subconscious mind'. In a balance to this comment, we could consider the highly popular *A Course in Miracles* – which was triggered by a series of visions, dreams and an inner voice that inspired the writing of the book – and might perhaps conclude that the quality of psychically and/or mystically written material cannot always be dismissed so easily.

But no matter what type of phenomena are being encountered, we need to reflect upon their validity and see if they are leading us and others to a healthy understanding of the sacredness of life. Our own wisdom needs to play a part. Phenomena should not override the importance of compassionate actions or the promotion of unity and peace with others and living skilfully and wisely in every moment. This requires an interspiritual and deep ecumenical approach to our unfoldment that wholesomely accepts we do not have all the answers and honours the spiritual teachings of others. I use the word 'spiritual' here to imply teachings and practices that unite instead of divide people and their shared responsibilities for each other and all Earth-life, of which we are amazing parts.

* * *

2
Yogis & Buddhas

The Powers in Hindu Spirituality

Yogins and yoginis tell us that astral beings are everywhere. To know this truth they must possess clairvoyant and other types of shamanistic and mediumistic abilities. When we look at early Yogic and Hindu spiritual traditions, we see that since early Vedic times, around the 2nd millennium BCE, there has been the belief in various extraordinary powers, including the power of specialised rituals and the creative use of prayer and mantra helping to maintain cosmic order (called *rita* in Sanskrit). Some scholars have speculated that these rituals and the belief in their results point towards an early understanding of creative karmic action having positive effects. However, other scholars have argued against this idea and believe the notion of karma (actions having consequences) and teachings about its connections with desires first appeared in the earliest Upanishads as an outside influence entering the Hindu tradition around 800 BCE.

Within various Hindu traditions (Hinduism is an umbrella term that is popularly used to describe a variety of Indian traditions that have numerous different links with each other), there is also the belief in what is called *tapas*, which literally means 'heat'. This goes back to the early Rig Veda, one of the oldest collections of hymns within Hinduism. *Tapas* reflects the Vedic idea of a God-force (Brahman) that is seen to reside in mantras and prayers and released when recited during specific rituals.

The generation of this mystical heat within oneself is thought to yield supernatural powers, called *siddhis* in the Yogic traditions, which roughly translates as 'perfect abilities' and were also called *prabhava*, 'excelling in power', in early teachings. Through fasting or other disciplines, a yogi can internally build the mystical heat of *tapas*, which unfolds psychic abilities. In the later Epic literature of the Hindu tradition (Mahabharata and Ramayana), *tapas* refers and is connected to the practice of extreme asceticism and its results, and as a power that can be transferred from a guru to a disciple. Here it is seen as a potent psychic force that is given to another in order to help him or her open to numerous subtle levels of being and move forward on numerous paths towards enlightenment.

There are various legends that mention some of the abilities of different yoga ascetics, such as the ancient story about how, through tapas, a yogi named Bhagiratta urged God to release the river Ganges, which was said to have originally only flowed in heaven and cause it to flow on Earth:

Bhagiratta kept his arms raised for a thousand years and stood on one leg for another thousand. When the Gods at last granted his request, the force of the water came pouring down.

~ FRITS STAAL

The divine being Krishna, who imparts profound teachings on Yoga to the warrior prince Arjuna on the eve of a great battle in the Bhagavad Gita, is renowned for various miracles and heroic deeds in numerous legends about him. He is not mentioned in the early Vedic teachings but has become one of the most revered figures in various Hindu traditions. Some scholars such as my previous university lecturer Professor Friedhelm Hardy thought he must have been an actual historical teacher who gained a popular following in order to appear suddenly on the scene and be written about with such devotion.

There are scores of legends about Krishna in the Bhagavata Purana, which describe him defeating numerous mythical beings and creatures. As a child, his adoptive mother Yashoda is said to have found the whole Universe inside of his mouth and as an adult he is said to have stopped the course of the sun to influence the outcome of a battle. He is also reported to have saved his village from the destruction of a giant snake by dancing on its head.

Powers of various kinds, performed by different teachers and masters are mentioned in an array of revered teachings, such as clairvoyance, telepathy, making oneself and objects invisible and the ability to leave the physical body at will and enter another body, even a dead body. In Swami Rama's autobiography, he mentions a yogi that is said to have done this in modern times. This ability, which is described in the Mahabharata (Anusasanaparvan 13:40-41) – the longest poem in the world with many key teachings on desires, personal duty and spiritual liberation – is looked upon as a special power obtained by yogis and is thought to be a side effect of overcoming attachment and bondage to the physical body and worldly experience.

Book Three of the classic Yoga Sutra teaches about various powers that can be developed through yoga practices. Once the practitioner has control over his or her consciousness, he or she reaches a particular stage of meditation where certain powers are acquired, such as memory of previous lives and knowing the cries/suffering of all creatures and the mental states of all people. These powers are the same as the superknowledges in Buddhism and are important features in both the Yoga Sutra and Buddhism for attaining liberation and spiritual freedom.

In the popular devotional text, the Bhagavata Purana, it describes the powers in detail and states there are 18 of them in all, whereas in contrast to this the Yoga Sutra lists as many as 30. Yet TS Rukmani informs us in an informative essay on the two texts that where the powers are acquired through one's own efforts in the Yoga Sutra, they are tied up with the notion of grace in the Bhagavata Purana and are given as a blessing to the devotee by God, the Lord of all *siddhis*. The power of omniscience, all-knowing, Rukmani tells us, comes to those whose minds are purified by devotion and know how to meditate on the divine Lord. All powers are seen to already exist in an infinite variety of forms in the divine and are given depending on the devotee's degree of dedication.

In the Bhagavata Purana, powers such as merging one's

consciousness with another's, entering another's body, dying at will, changing oneself into different physical forms and ultimate liberation itself, are all achieved by meditating on a particular aspect of God. Knowledge of other people's minds, Rukmani tells us, is said to unfold by meditating on ideas. However, knowledge of previous lives is not mentioned in the teachings. As well as this, Rukmani points out that the Bhagavata Purana does not grade the powers because they are tied up with corresponding aspects of God. Grading them would imply there are higher and lower aspects of the divine, which would be unacceptable to the teachers of the Bhagavata Purana.

The Yoga Sutra on the other hand, makes a distinction between major and minor powers. The most important being linked with the final stage of liberation. Namely, insight into distinguishing the difference between purified intelligence and wisdom (*sattvic* intelligence) and direct and ultimate knowledge of our authentic Self (*purusha* in the Yoga Sutra). Having insight into the ultimate reality of all things is of course looked upon as the highest gift in all mystical traditions. Yet each has their own unique understanding of its spiritual implications.

Connected with more harsh ascetic branches of Hindu Yoga are the legendary Nath yogis, who owe much to Tantric Yoga beliefs and practices:

> *The Naths or yogic 'Masters' are nine great adapts, of whom Siva himself is the first, parallel to the eighty-four immortal Siddhas of tantric Buddhism … [It] was through the Nath*

Yogins that tantric ideas and vocabulary became current among the masses between the twelfth and fifteenth centuries.

~ JL BROCKINGTON

What was said to distinguish the early Nath yogis from ordinary yoga practitioners was their power of control over death and decay. They were credited with having extensive occult powers that earned them a reputation as miracle workers.

Looking at Tantra and Kundalini Yoga we find a variety of practices being adopted in order to awaken what is described as the latent serpent/creative psychic power – termed *kundalini* – at the base of the spine and being able to raise it through various *nadis*/channels and energy points/*chakras* to reunite with *sahasrara* – described as 'the thousand petalled lotus' – at the crown of the head. It is said that when we are able to do this we experience the reunion of our individualised and universal cosmic nature, Shakti, the creative female energy, with the transcendent power of Shiva, symbolically seen as an unchanging male force standing outside time and causality. Neither of which are in fact seen as being superior to or separate from the other in Tantra:

Within Shiva there is Shakti; within Shakti there is Shiva. I see no difference between them; they are like the moon and the moon-light.

~ SIDDHASIDDHANTA SANGRAHA

It is also believed that through raising *kundalini* energy we are able to attain the *siddhis*. All these things are bound up with the idea of a subtle/psychic body that is mentioned in a variety of Yogic and philosophical teachings in Hindu traditions, which is connected with the vital *pranic* life force that permeates all things in the Universe. *Prana* itself is comparable to *chi* energy mentioned in Chinese traditions. Through practices such as breath control and focusing on the breath, which are essential parts of the yoga practice of *pranayama*, students are able to become more aware of *pranic* energy that works both within and around them and open to psychic and transforming spiritual levels of being and the powers these can bring.

However, practices of *pranayama* are not undertaken in isolation from other exercises. The influential, in Yogic circles, Yoga Sutra places such practices after the *yamas* (external ethical virtues) and *niyamas* (the cultivation of inner virtues), which include non-harmfulness, truthfulness and mindful introspection and conduct. As a whole, the *yamas* and *niyamas* are looked upon as indispensable practices in various Yogic traditions.

The Powers in Buddhist Spirituality

Many early Western interpreters of Buddhism saw the tradition essentially as a practical and ethical path to spiritual freedom. Any mention of supernormal powers was either overlooked or explained away as later interpolations. However, the Buddha was well aware that practices of meditation, which are seen as essential in his teachings for attaining enlightenment, led to possession of various powers. The following is what the eminent Buddhist scholar Hellmuth

Hecker pointed out about this in early Buddhist teachings:

> *The Pali suttas frequently ascribe supernormal powers to the Buddha and his arahant disciples, and there is little ground apart from personal prejudice for supporting such passages to interpolations ... [W]hen the suttas are considered in their totality, the clear conclusion emerges that the acquisition of paranormal powers was regarded as a positive good which serves to enhance the stature and completeness of the spiritually accomplished person.*

It has to be said the Buddha believed psychic or miraculous powers on their own had limited value – the true aim being to transcend the world of unsatisfactoriness (*duhkha*) – and even went as far to say he loathed the display of them in some of his teachings. Yet in the Digha Nikaya (1:213) there are accounts of him displaying a whole series of miraculous abilities, which he does in order to help his disciples in some way or to convert people, even though he would have normally converted his followers by preaching. One of the Buddha's main disciples Mahamggallana was credited with various remarkable gifts, including clairvoyance, clairaudience and telekinesis. In one story about him (Anguttara Nikaya 7:58) he is described as suffering from fatigue and how, by using his psychic powers, the Buddha was able to suddenly appear before him and make his drowsiness disappear.

Another account about the Buddha (Vinaya 1:24-34) mentions how he asked three fire worshipping brahmins if he could spend the night in a house where he was told there lived a supernatural *naga*/cobra that might burn him up. (There have even been accounts of these supernatural cobras reported in modern times and of revered Buddhist holy men and women such as Venerable Acariya Mun Bhuridatta Thera keeping them at bay.) The Buddha goes into the house and is unharmed and after a while he is described as generating heat and flames which are seen in five colours. The Buddha then performs various other miracles, after which the brahmins are said to throw away their fire worshipping equipment and convert to the Buddha's path.

Although an account such as this may well be meant to be interpreted allegorically to show the superiority of the Buddha and his path and can also be seen as an example of him using 'skill in means' (a particularly essential practice in the Buddhist tradition), the important point is that the display or mention of miracles and supernatural powers is there in the early literature and is a part of early Buddhism. What the Buddha normally objected to was the unnecessary display of such powers. For instance, in the Vinaya (2:110-2), which holds teachings for the monastic community, the Buddha rebukes the *bikkhu*/monk Pindola for demonstrating supernatural powers merely to impress the laity.

As mentioned previously, Buddhism also teaches about six superknowledges, termed *abhinna* in the ancient Pali language, the language of the early Theravada Buddhist teachings. The first five can all be classed as ordinary miraculous powers that are found in various Indian traditions and are bound up with the Buddha's teachings on meditation and identical with psychic powers found in Hindu traditions.

It is believed that through various practices of meditation we can easily develop the five superknowledges of Buddhism, which include the divine eye, the divine ear, remembrance of past lives, reading the thoughts of others and numerous other gifts such as seeing how the effects of previous karma influences people's rebirth. With the development of the divine ear, the Visuddhimagga (Theravada Buddhism's principal commentary on meditation practices) describes how one can hear the sounds/cries (the suffering) of both human and divine beings from a great distance as well as close-by.

Both the Samannaphala Sutta and the Visuddhimagga describe numerous other gifts, many of which are also found in Hindu spirituality, such as multiplying oneself many times, becoming invisible, walking through solid walls and mountains, diving in and out of the ground as though it were made of water, travelling through the sky (something the Buddha was said to have done), bilocation and producing a shower of water from the lower part of the body along with fire from the upper part.

The five superknowledges themselves are considered as being fairly mundane in Buddhist teachings and can be possessed by non-Buddhist masters of spirituality who have learned the art of meditation. Their display is not thought to imply that a true state of sanctity has been reached but can indeed indicate that a certain level of progress has been achieved. It is the sixth superknowledge, which is about knowledge of how we overcome inhibiting psychological traits and achieve freedom from binding and restrictive conditioning (*samsara*) that is the most valued.

Although aspects of the superknowledges can be thought of as subjective states encountered while meditating, rather than physical demonstrations of miracles, they are essential to the historical Buddha's teachings. In his own experiences towards enlightenment, he personally opened up to many of them before touching a pure unconditioned sublime state of awareness (Nirvana), after extinguishing desires, hatred and illusion. The powers themselves are not looked upon as harmful but as possible signs that an individual has suspended the laws of nature and overcome binding influences. But the Buddha warns us not to be tempted too much by them and so lose sight of the goal of liberation from birth, death and rebirth, and what he saw as other important areas of unfoldment such as helping others to overcome their suffering, which he also classified as a type of supernormal power.

An illustration of the Buddha's pragmatic approach to spirituality is found in an account of him meeting an ascetic who told him that after 25 years the path he was following had finally born fruit and was now able to cross the river he was sitting next to by walking on the water. The Buddha was obviously unimpressed by the amount of time the man had wasted and pointed out that he could have simply paid a ferryman one penny to take him across. Interestingly, to falsely claim possession of miraculous powers is one of four offenses that can lead to expulsion from the Buddhist monastic community and ranks alongside killing, stealing and sexual misconduct. This demonstrates how serious Buddhists monks are about the powers.

In Mahayana Buddhism, the Buddha himself is said to have come back after his death (his *paranirvana*) and give further teachings at Vultures' Peak in the Bihar region in India. A popular text and teaching within the tradition is the Abhidharmakosa of Vasubanbhu (written around 5th century CE), which gives an account of five powers that are attained in different ways: by meditation, by being inborn, by spells, by herbs or by activities.

In Tibetan Buddhism we find The Tibetan Book of the Dead mentioning that those who enter the *sidpa bardo* realm discover that they are endowed with the power of miraculous action (the ability to change shape, multiply oneself, become larger or smaller and disappear). This multifaceted ability is described as arising naturally. Though according to Evans-Wentz in his translation of the book, the desire for it Tibetan lamas say should be avoided until we are ready to use it and other supernatural abilities wisely.

The great Tibetan yogi Milarepa (1025-1135 CE) is reported to have possessed a number of psychic powers, including the ability to walk, rest and sleep while levitating. Various Tibetan ascetics are said to have produced spontaneous phenomena such as leaving impressions in solid rocks from where they had stood, sat or laid. In the meditation practice of *gTum-mo* monks have been well-documented in recent years to have generated heat in sub-zero temperatures and within minutes started to dry out dripping wet, ice-cold blankets placed over them, which is done to test the proficiency of monks in the practice.

The Vajrayana or Diamond Vehicle School of Buddhism,

which is also referred to as 'Mantrayana' because of the importance placed on mantra practices, is of particular interest. In this tradition the ability to employ a mantra properly requires knowledge of using special psychic powers:

[M]antra gives power only to those who are conscious of its inner meaning, acquainted with its methods of operation and who know that it is a means to call up the dormant forces within us, through which we are capable of directing our destiny and of influencing our surroundings.

~ LAMA ANAGARIKA GOVINDA

In recent years we have seen the Soka Gakkai branch of Buddhism claiming that by chanting before the *ghonzon* (a mandala inscribed with the words *namu myo-ho-renge-kyo*: 'Hail to the wonderful truth of the Lotus Sutra') has brought about such things as emotional and physical well-being, improved relationships with friends and family and in some cases has been said to have cured illnesses.

The Vajrayana tradition is acquainted with eight particular abilities, which represent various powers of mastery over the body, including such things as the elixir for the eyes that make the gods visible, the life-essence that preserves youth, fleetness in running and the ability to fly and have control over spirits and demons. In the biographies of the 84 male and female *mahasiddhas* preserved in the Tibetan tradition, the attainment of these abilities is described in detail.

The actual title of *mahasiddha* roughly means 'a great

master of perfect abilities' and refers to a practitioner who has mastered the teachings of the Tantras. A yogi in any Indian tradition who attains enlightenment may be given the title of *siddha*. But the fact that this term is connected with the word *siddhi* indicates that it is primarily a form of spiritual awakening that connects strongly with psychic and miraculous abilities. Yet as seen in both Buddhist and Hindu spirituality, enlightenment is looked upon as something different to other powers. Because of this, it is sometimes described as the *supreme siddhi*.

* * *

3
Prophets & Mystics

The Powers in Jewish Spirituality
One of the most fascinating things in the Jewish
scriptures is the mention of angels. They are looked
upon slightly differently but no less significant to how some
might think of them today, as the Hebrew term *malakh*,
meaning 'angel', is sometimes used in early sections of the
Bible to refer to beings who can take on human form to do
God's work or carry a message. For example, in the account
of the fall of Jericho, Joshua sees a man standing in front of
him claiming he is a commander of the Lord (Josh. 5:13-14).
Only later did the term come to be used more specifically
for non-physical beings from heavenly realms acting as God's
messengers. Gabriel and Michael are the only two angels
mentioned by name in the Hebrew Bible. Raphael and
Uriel are mentioned in the books of the Apocrypha, a later
collection of scriptures found in some Christian Bibles, which
are not in the Jewish canon. In the mystical teachings of the
Kabbalah an archangel is assigned to each emanation on the
Tree of Life.

The influential Jewish philosopher Maimonides (1135-1204 CE) believed that anyone entrusted with a mission was an angel. Implying that any person who had been touched by divinity and had been inspired to help humanity in some way could be looked upon as having an angelic nature. Though modern Jewish teachings do not deny the existence of angels, biblical passages that refer to them are generally thought of as more symbolic and poetic.

One can see how the belief in angels continued in both the Christian and Islamic traditions. Similar to modern-day Spiritualists' beliefs, some Catholics believe in a personal guardian angel though Spiritualists would usually prefer the term 'spirit guide'. The Islamic faith mentions four particular archangels – Izrail, the angel of death, who is not actually referred to by name in the Qur'an, Israfil, the angel who will announce the Day of Judgment, Gabriel, the angel who brings divine revelation to people's hearts, and Michael, who holds important status with Gabriel – along with the angels Munkar and Nakir who question people on their first night in the grave about the Prophet Muhammad. In the Old Testament, Michael is the guardian angel of Israel.

Angels in the more traditional sense of the word are obviously seen as special beings and the ability to be aware of and be in contact with them could be considered as a form of clairvoyant, clairaudient or clairsentient ability. On the whole, the Bible looks upon the activity of angels as an assurance of God's involvement in the world. Their appearance often signifies God's presence. In fact, some passages where it refers to 'the angel of the Lord' (thought to be a special angel), it is hard to know if it is the actual presence of God or a separate agent being mentioned, as seen in Genesis, Chapter 16 (9-13), where it uses the phrase and also mentions seeing God.

As well as angels, both the Old and New Testament make numerous references to the significance of dreams and their meanings, which were also seen as important to the early Church fathers, including St Augustine. Further to this there are various well-known nature miracles reported in the Book of Exodus such as a strong wind that famously caused the Red Sea to part (14:21). Elsewhere there is mention of fire that is said to have fallen from the Lord to consume burnt offerings (1 Kgs. 18:37-38) and manna/food appearing at a time when the Israelites were wandering in the desert and in need of nourishment (Exod. 16:26-36). But it is difficult to say exactly how hungry the Israelites could have been as they were only into the second month of their escape from Egypt and had taken dough for unleavened bread and large droves of livestock with them (Exod. 12:34-38).

It has been speculated that manna may have been something that was secreted by insects or grew on tamarisk trees, which is known to have a sweet taste. But no matter how natural to the area it may have been, it was the way that it synchronisticly played its part in being there just when the Israelites were in need of food to sustain them that is looked upon as miraculous.

There are various other miraculous events mentioned in Hebrew scriptures, including three accounts of people being raised from the dead. Two of these were remarkably performed in similar ways by the prophets Elijah and Elisha

(1 Kgs. 17:21-22 and 2 Kgs. 4:32-35), and the other by a dead man's body being thrown into the grave of Elisha and coming into contact with his bones (2 Kgs. 13:20-21).

Additionally, the Hebrew Bible contains numerous prophecies. A prophet it ought to be said is someone who is believed to have been appointed by God to spread God's message or teachings – sometimes reluctantly, as seen in the account of Moses and his ministry – or motivated by a higher justice to take action and protect the rights of those without a public voice. They are people who are often moved with the help of divine inspiration to act compassionately and speak out in times of great social injustice. Examples of such people in the 20th century are Mahatma Gandhi and Martin Luther King Jr, and more recently the activist, physicist and ecologist Vandana Shiva has done much in the fight for eco-justice in India.

Yet the early Hebrew prophets are not remembered because of the accuracy of any predictions they made as they were sometimes wrong. In Isaiah there is an insistence that the city of Jerusalem would never be taken by a foreign enemy (though it has to be said that some biblical scholars believe the prophecies in Isaiah are not the product of a single author). What is seen as more important are the revelations that encourage the Israelites to find spiritual freedom or remind them to repent their sins and cease worshipping false gods and idols. But the idea of sin needs to be made clear here. For the majority of people of the Jewish faith hold no concept of original sin, which is a relatively late doctrine of the Christian Church that was not accepted until the 5th century CE, after being developed by St Augustine (354-

430 CE). Instead, our original nature is seen as good and life and Creation are viewed as divine gifts from God. A young child's nature is held up as innocent and pure. A concept that is also held in the Islamic tradition, the Christian Orthodox Church and by many progressive Christians.

The central focus of the message and teachings of the prophets in the Hebrew Bible is generally concerned with encouraging individuals and/or the Israelites as a whole to keep to and follow a path of righteousness. The prophecies also tell of forthcoming events and give general warnings and comfort. Many of the early prophets gave their prophecies in ecstatic states, in which it was believed the spirit of Yahweh/God possessed and spoke through them. Through this activity they were then able to guide the early Israelites.

Other Old Testament and Jewish biblical prophecies mention the coming of the Messiah, who even today members of the faith believe will not come until the Second Temple in Jerusalem is rebuilt. At various times up to the present some have tried to relate biblical prophecies concerning the future to their own times, with the belief that such things can never be wrong. Yet it has been shown that what such people are often doing is predicting after an event, which is technically known as 'retroactive clairvoyance'. Liberal thinkers of both the Jewish and Christian faith accept this view. Additionally, many passages of the Bible are open to all kinds of interpretation and we can arguably read just about anything into them if we put our minds to it.

In looking at the different areas of phenomena there can be a danger in focusing purely on them and overlooking the unshakable foundations of the Jewish faith, which are primarily concerned with the preservation of life,* justice, the making of a better world and acting righteously and compassionately towards others and what those with spiritual vision have to say to us today about their tradition's teachings.

Hillel, one of the most important figures in Jewish history, who lived in Jerusalem during the time of King Herod, was once asked to summarise the whole of the Torah whilst standing on one leg, to which he replied, 'That which is hateful to you, do not do to others'. The highly influential contemporary rabbi Michael Lerner encourages us to seek to connect our lives with the unfolding of the Spirit in the Cosmos with the creative healing and transforming energy of the Universe and to touch our authentic spiritual nature and realise it is a manifestation of the ultimate divine presence in all. In his excellent book *Spirit Matters*, he describes how the greatest joy in life comes from being able to recognise ourselves as a part of the unity of All Being and seeing that we are manifestations of love, goodness, joy and creativity. For all life, he passionately and movingly reminds us, is ultimately filled with Spirit.

Symbolically connected with unity and creativity are the two interlocking triangles of the Jewish Star of David – a popular symbol in many cultures – which represent the joining

---

* Note: The notion of stewardship found in Judaism, Christianity and Islam, *some believe* needs reassessing as it is seen to place humans above other species and implies that nature requires us humans to have control over the natural world instead of learning how to live more closely in harmony with her and find mutually beneficial enrichment.

of two worlds, male and female energies coming together and the overcoming of opposites. Thus representing harmony and unity and the integration of creative qualities.

The Powers in Christian Spirituality

Within the Christian tradition, numerous miracles can be traced back to Jesus and the Old Testament. There is a tendency for some to think of Jesus as either a mystic or a medium with great healing abilities. But we must remember that for the majority of Christians, Jesus is neither of these as he is looked upon more through the eyes of John's Gospel and the resolution made by the First Council of Nicaea in 325 CE as God (as part of the Christian Trinity). Some Hindus also believe this as they consider Jesus to be an *avatar*, a divine incarnation. This belief may sit uncomfortably with some. But if we are to live harmoniously in pluralistic societies with people holding different beliefs, there needs to be an acceptance of difference where we agree to disagree and respect others' paths and seek out common ground where we can share the deeper mysteries and practices of an authentic spirituality.

Much is popularly known about the miracles of Jesus such as curing those who were blind, sick or lame, bringing Lazarus back to life, calming a storm, walking on water and turning water into wine. His miracles were seen by some of his followers to be signs that he was the expected Messiah and that God's new kingdom was about to come. However, for some Christians his miracles are not looked upon for authenticating his status as according to Matthew's Gospel Jesus refused to perform them for that purpose (12:38-39).

Yet John's Gospel mentions Jesus performing seven signs that show him to be the one who has come from heaven to provide eternal life. But it is perhaps the way in which he is said to have both entered and left the world that are thought to be the most miraculous events in his life.

Jesus's virgin birth is told differently in two of the four canonical Gospels. It is also told differently in the Muslim Qur'an, which credits the infant Jesus with the ability to speak. It seems extraordinary that what is seen to be an important event by many Christians is not mentioned in the Mark or John Gospels – the beginning of John's Gospel associates Jesus with the divine Logos and mentions how the Word was made flesh, and there is only a scant reference to Jesus's mother in Mark 6:3, of which neither mention anything about a virgin birth – and raises questions as to whether it was something that was added to Matthew's and Luke's Gospels in an attempt to give more weight to Jesus's importance. There has also been some research into Jesus's human birth being deliberately played down as there were some who wanted to see him as solely divine. In Bart D Ehrman's *Jesus, Interrupted* he mentions how the writer of Matthew's Gospel is drawing on a prophetic saying by the Hebrew prophet Isaiah about a 'young woman' conceiving (*alma* in Hebrew), which Ehrman points out 'came to be rendered into the Greek word for virgin (*parthenos*), and that is the form of the [translation of the Hebrew] Bible that [the author of] Matthew read'.

Not all Christians believe in the virgin birth of course – see John Shelby Spong's book *Born of a Woman: A Bishop*

Rethinks the Virgin Birth and the Treatment of Women by a Male-Dominated Church – and accept that the retelling of a holy man or woman's life can become more embellished and elaborated over the years. Many important figures in the past such as Alexander the Great and the Buddha were also credited with virgin births. Interestingly, the Gospel of Thomas and the contents of the speculated lost Q Gospel – the letter Q is an abbreviation of the German word *quelle* meaning 'source' – focus more on Jesus's teachings rather than on his life and deeds. In recent years, the Episcopal priest Cynthia Bourgeault has also written about Jesus being a great wisdom teacher.

The accounts of Jesus's resurrection is a different matter and is recorded in all of the four canonical Gospels, but each gives a different account of what actually happened. In Chapter 28 of Matthew's Gospel it describes how Mary Magdalene and the 'other Mary' find Jesus's tomb empty and how an angel tells them that Jesus has risen, after which they meet Jesus on their way to tell the apostles what had just happened. Though perhaps we should say 'other apostles' if we accept the view of the Gospel of Mary Magdalene, which sees her as one of the main and most important disciples with secret teachings of Jesus and fitting the role of an apostle herself. What the Gospels show us is that Mary Magdalene is in fact 'an apostle to the apostles' as she is described as the first (John's Gospel) or amongst the first to bring them news about Jesus's resurrection – in the synoptic Gospels she is *divinely appointed* to tell the male disciples this. In 2016 the Vatican officially recognised this important role of Mary's.

The oldest of the canonical Gospels is now thought to be

Mark's Gospel, of which the original ended at Chapter 16, Verse 8. Verses 9-20 were added later. Mark describes how Mary Magdalene and Mary the mother of James, and Salome, find the tomb empty and meet a young man in white who informs them that Jesus has risen.

In Chapter 24 of Luke's Gospel, Cleopas, who is someone we know nothing about, and another disciple are the first to be mentioned as seeing Jesus, and there are several women, including Mary Magdalene, who go to the tomb, find it empty and are met there by two men wearing shining clothes who ask them why they are 'looking for the living amongst the dead'.

In Chapter 20 of John's Gospel, only Mary Magdalene is said to have gone to the tomb and found it empty. After this she tells Simon Peter and the disciple Jesus loved, who then make their way to the tomb to see for themselves. It is only once they have gone back to where they were staying that Mary Magdalene then sees two angels in white who ask her why she is crying and then sees Jesus, who tells her not to hold onto to him as he has not yet returned to his Father.

The contradictions in the four Gospel accounts obviously make us wonder just how much of them are reliable. But we have to remember they cannot be read in exactly the same way as contemporary historical documents of events although some Christians try to do this. They are testaments of faith and can also be compared to ways in which people remember things differently today about events that have happened. Modern-day police are only too aware of the latter when taking notes from witnesses at crime scenes. But the Bible's written Gospels are not *direct* eye-witness accounts as the stories were first shared orally over a period of time before being written down in Greek. In addition to this, the term 'resurrection' is symbolic language and can mean different things to different people. The finding of the empty tomb and Mary Magdalene's involvement as a chief witness are the only consistent elements.

In analysis, the question has to be asked as to whether an empty tomb implies that Jesus's physical body was actually resurrected or not. (Interestingly there are stories of Tibetan yogis and lamas whose bodies are said to have disappeared on their death.) Some biblical scholars believe the fact that women are featured so heavily in the Gospel accounts adds validity to them, as prejudice towards women in Jesus's time shows they were not usually looked upon as reliable witnesses in places such as a Jewish court of law. Therefore, if someone was to fabricate a story of this kind during that period and wanted to convince others about its credibility, he or she would not have included women as central eye-witnesses, especially someone with Mary Magdalene's possibly implied troublesome past. However, Bart D Ehrman points out in *How Jesus Became God* that we are not talking about a Jewish lawcourt but an oral tradition in which women were well-represented in its early years and played crucial roles ministering as deacons, leading services in their homes and engaging in missionary activities.

Coming back to Mary Magdalene, we are not told exactly what was wrong with her, although Luke's Gospel tells us that seven demons were cast out of her (8:2), which could simply mean she was suffering from such things as depression or too much pride but then became more spiritually whole and balanced. She is, however, one of Jesus's closest and most devoted followers. The idea of her being a prostitute is now accepted as a later misinterpretation of the Gospel texts that was done deliberately to underplay the important role of women in the early Jesus movement. Many now consider the historical Jesus to have been an early feminist because of his inclusive attitude towards women. Also, in the original Greek language that Romans was written in, Paul describes Andronicus and Junia as the foremost among the apostles (16:7). Junia is a female name which seems to have been deliberately translated into the male name Junius in many English translations.

Jesus's famous saying, 'I and the Father are One' (John 10:30) is his most fascinating statement. For some Christians it is thought to confirm his special divine status – in Elaine Pagels' *Beyond Belief* she mentions that in the Jewish tradition in biblical times the titles 'Son of God' and 'Messiah' that are connected to Jesus and have come to imply his unique divinity in various Christian circles, would have designated someone who was Israel's human king. For others, Jesus's saying is seen as being no different to the insights of various mystics who realised in the deepest depth of their being there is a supreme sacred oneness that connects us with all life. This corresponds more with the teachings of the Gospel of Thomas, which encourage us to realise that the kingdom of God is both within and all around us. Interestingly, some texts such as the Thomas Gospel are sometimes referred to as 'apocryphal'. Although this word has come to imply an unreliable source of reference, it has its roots in the Greek language and actually means 'hidden' or 'secret'. Implying that the teachings are meant to be understood more esoterically.

Jesus's transfiguration, where it is said his face shone like the sun and his clothes became as white as light (Matt. 17:2) or a flash of lightening (Luke 9:28) has become a popular episode in his life for some Spiritualists to identify with. There are indeed some parts of the event that are comparable to Spiritualistic types of physical phenomena such as the materialisation of the deceased Moses and Elijah (Matt. 17:3 and Luke 9:30) and a discarnate voice that spoke to Peter, James and John (Matt. 17:5). The mention of a bright cloud that enveloped them (Matt. 17:2) was speculated by James F Malcolm to possibly be ectoplasm. But as so little information is given about this cloud we cannot really say what it was or why it was there.

Another episode in the life of Jesus shows him having the ability to foretell his own arrest, which can be seen in Matthew's Gospel where he tells his disciples he will be betrayed by one of them (26:21). Controversially the Gnostic Gospel of Judas has raised some questions about whether Jesus planned his own death or not, even though the idea of martyrdom is not advocated in the text. Ideas held by many Christians about Jesus's crucifixion and death being an act of atonement or bringing about salvation for humanity, which draws on passages in Corinthians, and the Mark and John Gospels, has some similarities with a practice found in Yogic traditions where a guru may voluntarily take on the karma of a disciple or community in order to advance their spiritual evolvement.

In some ways I find it more fascinating to look at the lives of those who came after Jesus, as here we find people with *almost* similar status to ourselves, instead of having the title of being the saviour of all humanity attached to their importance, who are trying to make sense of the spiritual life and how to assess the use of various gifts that can unfold. Jesus after all said that those who believed in him would do even greater things than he did (John 14:12), so let us look at what some of these things might be...

If we focus on the life of Paul we find he is presented as a great miracle worker in the Acts of the Apostles and is credited with the power of healing. He is said to have performed exorcisms and cured a man who was sick with fever and dysentery by laying his hands upon him (Acts 28:8). In Paul's letters to the Corinthians, it clearly shows that various gifts were part of early Christian experience and gives detailed instructions about the use of various abilities such as prophecy, healing and speaking in tongues. The latter first happened within the early Jesus movement at the Feast of Pentecost after Jesus's death, where a sound like a violent wind came from heaven and what is described as looking like tongues of fire rested on the apostles and other followers of Jesus and they began to speak in other languages (Acts 2:1-12). Rightly or wrongly this event is often looked upon as the beginning of the Christian Church by many Christians, but not all. However, Paul warns about special gifts and mentions that if one has the gift of prophecy for example or a faith that can move mountains but does not have love, one has nothing (1 Cor. 13:1-3).

Later the practice of speaking in tongues was seen to be heretical by the established Church, but it has never died out completely. It was actually considered as a divine gift by some saints who possessed or knew about others with the ability, whose very lives were seen to illustrate that it must have been given by God. However, today the Catholic Church in particular is generally suspicious of the ability to speak in a language of which one has no prior knowledge.

If we look at the lives of some of the great Christian mystics, we find various visions and other types of phenomena persistently appearing. Teresa of Avila (1515-1582) was said to have levitated several times and frequently had visions of angels. In one particular vision she experienced, which many academics have noticed has sexual overtones – which mystical experiences can have in relation to the idea of union – an angel manifested holding a spear of gold. At the tip of the spear there appeared to be a small fire. The angel then thrust the spear into her heart and then withdrew it. The experience left Teresa feeling as though she was on fire and was immediately overwhelmed with a great feeling of love.

While praying on the mountain of Verna, Francis of Assisi (1181-1226) is reported to have had a vision of a seraph, a six-winged angel, on a cross that pierced him with the stigmata, the five wounds of Jesus. Other stigmatists such as Padre Pio (1887-1968) and Therese Neumann (1898-1962) are reported to have had abilities of healing and bilocation and to have performed various other miracles. Sometimes people witnessed a perfume emanating from Padre Pio, especially the odour of violets, lilies, roses and incense, even though as a Capuchin monk he would obviously not have worn perfume. This phenomenon was seen as a sign that God had bestowed some grace on those who noticed it.

What comes over in the lives of the great mystics of the Catholic Church is that they do not seek to attain supernatural gifts. Nor do they encourage others to possess them as they are seen as divine blessings that are given by God. Teresa of Avila even advised beginners that it was best to resist them, believing the soul will advance quicker for doing so. The emphasis is more on the practice of contemplation, prayer and spiritual conduct.

Nonetheless, although it appears that they do not seek the gifts, there are many accounts of them using them once they have manifested. Teresa's spiritual life and career as an abbess were governed by the voices she heard. The voices even warned her of coming events. Similarly, the medieval mystic Hildegarde of Bingen experienced various mystical visions throughout her life as an abbess, which guided her in the affairs of her convent. Similar to the accounts of Jesus, Padre Pio is said to have stroked the eyes of a young child and cured her blindness and to have helped a cripple to walk without the aid of crutches. On one occasion he told a woman he had dispelled the devil away from her. But John of the Cross warned that the gifts can be used wrongly to deceive people and believed that there were some that were true and some that were not. Jesus also warned that, 'Impostors will come claiming to be messiahs or prophets, and they will produce great signs and wonders to mislead' (Matt. 24:24).

On the whole Catholic mystics appear unanimous in warning against attributing too much importance to the gifts. In chapter three of *The Ascent of Mount Carmel*,

John of the Cross wrote that joy in supernatural gifts and graces – what he termed 'the fifth class of goods' – must be directed to God. He believed, as did Paul, that they are given for the benefit of others and that joy in them should be avoided. People he felt should rejoice not in the possession and exercise of the gifts themselves but should seek and rejoice in the benefits of being able to serve God through them. More than anything, he believed charity was the more precious fruit of spiritual life.

This slightly negative view about possession of any gifts is given to encourage a sense of humility, though as can be seen, the idea of having joy in them is not completely lacking. There is nothing wrong with humility of course, but I feel there is equally nothing wrong with having a sense of awe and joyousness in the things that unfold on spiritual paths. The contemporary writer on Creation-Centred Spirituality, Matthew Fox, also encourages us to find a sense of awe and joy in the array of gifts we have, including those we may take for granted such as the gifts of parenthood, kindness and friendship.

On the subject of visions, whether objective or sub-jective, the Christian author Albert Farges pointed out the importance of examining them for clearness and detail: to distinguish between that which comes from nature, from God, from the imagination or the devil, though most Christians would not believe in the devil these days. If we put the latter into contemporary terms, we might think of the devil as a symbolic metaphor for shadow parts of ourselves – as parts that can stop us from growing, being inclusive and realising our full creative and compassionate potential. Those who actually believe in a demonic realm invariably use it as a way of projecting the shadow parts of their psychological selves onto others, instead of owning and working with and transforming them and becoming more all-embracingly open to life and accepting of others.

Farges believed that genuine visions should appear spontaneously without preparation and disappear in the same manner. I can only assume he believed this as it would make less room for a vision to be coloured by our imagination. But contemporary psychological discoveries show how our unconscious mind influences much of conscious experience, whether in a spontaneous mode or not.

Farges mentions two types of visions: clear and obscure. The obscure transcends ordinary imagery, which ties in with experiences found in other traditions where mystics are often lost for words to describe things beyond everyday realms of experience. The clear reminds us how many mystical openings are intensely vivid and seem more dynamically real than regular perceptions. There is no loss of lucidity or vagueness about them when awakened to and experienced. Instead, they seem to bring about a wider understanding of the reality and sacredness of all.

For many Christian mystics, the experience of clairvoyant visions and clairaudient voices are seen as stages that may happen in their lives. Interestingly, the Orthodox Church even uses the terms 'clairvoyant' and 'clairaudient'. But there are other stages where what is sometimes called the 'mystic death' (often seen as the death of the individual 'I' or ego, but a healthier view might be to consider it as a stage where the limitations of our individual self are overcome, rather than a complete annihilation of it) or the 'dark night of the soul' occurs, where mystics are not always aware of any divine voice or visionary experience. In many ways Baptism can be seen as a ritual enactment of this stage on the mystical journey, where one dies, symbolically, and becomes a new person. It may seem like a spiritually dry period that is seldom lit by any uplifting experience, but it is looked upon as a stage of progression and purification that can happen before a profound awareness of supreme unitive consciousness is awakened to, where the soul loses its separateness in the pure bliss and love of the divine.

The renowned 20th century writer on Christian mysticism Evelyn Underhill believed that mystical visions and the hearing of mystical voices had a life-enhancing quality about them and were the means through which one truly approached God. In other words, they are not only necessary phenomena for seeking union with the divine but are important experiences that bring about positive changes in an individual's spiritual growth:

They infuse something new in the way of strength, knowledge, direction; and leave it – physically, mentally, or spiritually – better than they found it.

~ EVELYN UNDERHILL

In addition to this, Elaine Pagels, who has written much about Gnostic Christianity, points out that, 'Without visions and revelations … the Christian movement would not have begun'. She even speculates whether,

Those who wrote, translated, and carefully copied works such as the Secret Book of James and the Prayer of the Apostle Paul may have known about techniques that Jewish groups used to induce a state of ecstasy and invoke visions ... Some of the Dead Sea Scrolls also offer prayers and rituals apparently intended to help the devout enter God's presence and join in worship with angels.

The Powers in Islamic Spirituality

The Qur'an, which literally means 'the recital', is held to be the direct word of God by Muslims and is the most sacred book of the Islamic faith. It is said to have been revealed by the angel Gabriel to the Prophet Muhammad while in various meditative trance-like states over a period of approximately 20 years, until the latter part of his life. The official Islamic accounts of Muhammad's life (570-632 CE) say that he first encountered this experience in the 7th century CE when he was about 40 years old while meditating in a cave on the outskirts of Makkah. The Qur'an itself is looked upon by Muslims as a word for word translation of a tablet that is eternally preserved in heaven.

The Qur'an does not use the word miracle but instead mentions the Arabic word *ayat*, meaning 'signs'. The Qur'an is in fact considered to have been created in a miraculous way – as a divine revelation. Because of this, it is referred to and looked upon as a miracle itself. Some Muslims have claimed that the Prophet Muhammad was actually illiterate and that this adds more weight to the claim of their principal Holy Book being a miracle. Even if man and *jinn*, a fiery spirit personality in Islam that is believed to be a separate species to angels and humans, banded together to try to produce it they would not be able to, the Qur'an tells us (17:90).

Although the Qur'an is seen as the principal miracle that happened in the life of the Prophet, various Hadiths, which contain his sayings and numerous legends about him, attribute many other miracles to him such as splitting the moon on one occasion when the people of Makkah requested to see a miracle. It seems like a particularly improbable claim if taken literally and was not reported to have been seen anywhere else in the world, which would be expected if such an event had happened, though it has a certain amount of charm about it. Yet it is surprisingly similar to a passage found in Buddhist scriptures about internal unity, which mentions how, 'A monk who is skilled in concentration can cut the Himalayas in two' (Anguttara Nikaya 6:24).

There are accounts of the Prophet multiplying water and food on different occasions. Once there was not enough water for ritual washing before prayer time. Muhammad put his hand inside a vessel that contained only a small amount of water and then spread out his fingers. Water then gushed out like a fountain for everyone to use. There are other miracles and miraculous events that are said to have happened around Muhammad and performed by him such as the restoring of a blind man's sight, and rocks and mountains being heard to speak and pay tribute to Muhammad.

But it is perhaps the Prophet's miraculous night journey, the *miraj*, that is the most fascinating. *Sura*/section 17.1 in the Qur'an mentions how he was transported from the town of

Makkah to the furthest place of worship and was shown various signs. Different Hadiths mention how Muhammad was taken to Jerusalem where he then ascended to heaven accompanied by the angel Gabriel. There he conversed with Moses, saw various other prophets such as Jesus and Abraham, and was given the obligatory prayers for the followers of the faith. Afterwards, he was then taken back to Makkah. The famous Dome of the Rock in Jerusalem is said to mark the exact spot where he ascended to heaven. Scholars and Muslims alike have adopted different standpoints about this significant event. Some have interpreted it as a dream that the Prophet had, while others believe it was actually his physical body or at the very least his spirit body that was transported to both Jerusalem and heaven. Michael Muhammad Knight believes that,

> *The ascension not only stakes an Islamic claim over other traditions, but also becomes a template for any mystic's journey, telling us about the capacity for all humans to embark on quests for transcendent encounters and advanced knowledge … In Sufi traditions, we find visionaries giving accounts of their own ascensions, recalling the various angelic, prophetic, or even divine figures with whom they interacted and the special secrets that they brought back to humankind.*

In considering the overall teachings of the Qur'an we ought to remember that they are not trying to promote a new religion but are looked upon by Muslims as a continuation of the older Judeo-Christian tradition. The teachings accept the Torah, the Gospels, the early Jewish prophets and Jesus as early revelation, although they attempt to undermine further prophetic insights by claiming Muhammad to be 'the Seal of the Prophets' (33:40), the last in the line of prophets linking with the Bible. But some Islamic scholars such as Wilfred Madelung thought that the meaning of the term was not so certain.

Even within the Islamic tradition there has been some careful wordplay used to subtly attempt to steer around the statement and what it is thought to imply, which can be seen in an idea about 'the Seal of the Saints' put forward by Ibn 'Arabi (1165-1240 CE), one of Sufism's – the main mystical branch of Islam – greatest teachers, in which he sees himself as being the last to receive esoteric teachings because of his spirit being identical with Muhammad's. But this idea actually contradicts 'Arabi's own teachings about One Essence, in which everyone's spirit is seen as identical and, therefore, there should be no reason why 'Arabi's spirit would be more special than or favoured over anyone else's.

Another important Sufi was Hallaj who was executed in Baghdad in 922 CE. He was associated with numerous miraculous abilities. He studied with the renowned Sufi Junayd in Iraq but broke away after a quarrel about following the path of the heart (called the Drunken School in Sufism) rather than the head (the Sober School) and later became a popular figure in Iran. He personally preferred to follow the path of devotion to God. He stopped wearing the woollen garment of the early Sufis and began to preach in public, as well as travel to places such as India and Central Asia.

He was eventually accused of performing magic and

miracles and was arrested and thrown into prison. It is said that some accused him of blasphemy and others accused him of being a secret Christian. Some lesser open-minded Sufis accused him of believing that both human and divine nature could be harmonised. In addition to this, others felt that an idea he held about incarnation was not acceptable, as it implied having two separate essences that could be united. For if you are already God in essence, which some of his sayings appear to have suggested, then you cannot *become* what you *already are*.

The main reason for his execution it seems was more to do with his teaching that the pilgrimage to Makkah could be done in one's own home and shows a lack of tolerance for different views and freethinking starting to enter the Islamic faith. His execution sent shockwaves through the Sufi tradition and put many of them on their guard. According to reports, the miracles were genuine and ranged from apporting fruit to making his whole body fill an entire room. Similar to Jesus, a popular saying of his was, 'I am the Truth, I am the Real', which draws on a famous saying in Islam. The divine is often referred to as 'the Real' in Sufism. In many ways Hallaj exemplified the deepest possibilities of personal piety to be found in Islam. He demonstrated the true meaning of submission to the unity of the divine – not with the aim of gaining any form of personal sanctity, but in order to live and teach the deeper mysteries of an authentic devotional life.

In the biographies of Islamic saints and mystics, there are accounts of both men and women who penetrated divine truths through their devotion to a spiritual way of life and living. The many miracles that have been credited to them are a part of mainstream Islamic belief. The Aqida Tahawi, which is a summary of Sunni beliefs, mentions the marvels of the saints and affirms the stories about them. Similar to the powers of Jesus and various yogis, their saints are credited with being able to fly, walk on water, foretell the future and travel hundreds of miles in one step.

In modern times we could draw upon one of the world's leading exponents of Islamic science and spirituality, Seyyed Hossein Nasr, who points out that Oneness is the highest of all experience and gifts, and how in its ultimate sense this belongs only to God as the absolute, which he universally describes as Brahman, Allah, the Godhead and as the highest and ultimate reality. His writings on Sufism have a contemporary feel about them, are all-embracing and focus on a profound spirituality that is about how it is only the Spirit that is able to bring about an integration and unity of the psyche, intellect and mind. This implies both a vertical transcendence in order to discover the divine and an embodiment of it that horizontally embraces divinity in our lives and exhibits natural acts of compassion as a result of this discovery:

The supreme formula for unity in Islam is that 'There is no Divinity but God'. That the Divine is all, in all and transcends all. The ultimate practice for Sufi's is not to pray at all times, but for one's life to become a constant act of prayer. For God is always present in all things.

~ SEYYED HOSSEIN NASR

*   *   *

73

4
Bringing the Strands Together

I t can be seen that each tradition takes a slightly different stand about miraculous powers and how they manifest, and even within each tradition there is a diversity of views. On the one hand, Catholic mystics do not aim to attain the gifts. For if they are gifts from God and seen as a sign of divine grace, then they can only be acquired as a gift, instead of personally developing them. On the other hand, Paul advocated the desire for spiritual gifts, especially prophecy (1 Cor. 14:1). The superknowledges in Buddhism along with the *siddhis* in the Yoga Sutra are nonetheless attained through one's own efforts and aimed for in order to help overcome the effects of various inhibiting *samskaras* (unconscious traits that affect various states of being) and achieve liberation. Though some of the powers appear to be more by-products of certain practices in the Yoga Sutra.

According to Swami Prabhavananda and Christopher Isherwood, Aphorism 321 of the Yoga Sutra recommends giving up the *siddhis* if we wish to attain liberation from the ties that bind us. This is a popular view that some hold. That only by renouncing the powers is a yoga practitioner able to achieve the higher spiritual goal and has arisen from a belief in the world being an illusion (*maya*) by some non-dualistic teachers of Hindu philosophy and, therefore, anything belonging to the world, including the *siddhis*, has little value. This is in fact a misleading interpretation of the Yoga Sutra and has created some uninformed prejudice in some circles. The idea of seeing everything as an illusion is also a dangerous belief if taken to the extremes of seeing nothing as valid or real in life, as it can lead to a lack of care for oneself, the Earth and others.

Although mystics and contemporary scientists both tell us that life is not as it appears, i.e. as being made up of individual separate life and phenomena, it does not imply that everyday experience does not have a level of reality and should not be a part of spiritual life. The great Vedantist philosopher Shankara (788-820 CE), whose teachings influenced many ideas about life as an illusion in Hinduism, drew upon the analogy of seeing a rope as a snake. If we think about this analogy, we see that it is more about misperceptions and not seeing things as they really are, which does not then imply that nothing is real and everything is an illusion.

In contrast to Prabhavananda and Isherwood's comment about the *siddhis*, the translation by JH Woods describes the same passage of the Yoga Sutra as being about 'having no cause for attachment or pride'. The excellent and always practical Yoga writer and practitioner Georg Feuerstein pointed out in his translation of the Sutra that, 'The popular opinion that these yogic abilities are not part of the path to Self-realisation is demonstrably wrong … they *cannot* be separated from the essentially organic and unitary structure of Yoga'.

Elsewhere in the Hindu tradition, although popular devotional texts such as the Bhagavata Purana tell us that the *siddhis* are 'given by God', instead of being developed through practices, they can be seen to be partly earned through one's own efforts, as the devotee has to deliberately meditate on a feature of God to have them bestowed upon him or her. However, it should be mentioned that the powers are not primarily sought after or given for the attainment of mastery over the elements but for mastery over ourselves. This view seems to apply to all of the Yogic traditions. For it is the attainment of spiritual freedom and not the actual powers themselves that indicates authentic progress.

According to the religious studies scholar Mircea Eliade 'he who succumbs to the desire to use them ultimately remains a mere "magician," without power to surpass himself'. But contrary to this, it can be seen that having been attained the powers are often used in different spiritual traditions. Christian mystics believe they can be used as a way of service to God. Ancient brahmin priests used their powers in the belief that they were helping to maintain cosmic order. The Buddha used them for the purpose of conversion and on the nights of his enlightenment. Even today Buddhists and Hindus sometimes seek help from a teacher whose compassion for humanity in conjunction with his or her special gifts might be called upon to benefit others in their community. Plus, the belief in the power of prayer in all religions is held by millions of people throughout the world.

Why some yogis such as Gopi Krishna advocated not using the gifts, especially as it can be seen that some of them are used in order to become aware of unconscious influences (*samskaras*) and help undo the effects of binding karma, may well be because they wanted to focus people's attention more on the spiritual dimensions of their tradition rather than on the sensational. I do not see reasons why those naturally endowed with gifts of healing, for example, should need to deny or suppress them as not only would it create a psychological imbalance, but it would also stop them from co-operating with the creative divine mind of the Universe. Would it not be better to use all gifts we have selflessly and wisely and allow them to lead us to a wider understanding of spirituality? Where all traditions appear to agree is in warning that miraculous powers should not be sought for their own sake or be used to reinforce our self-importance.

The emphasis for taking a spiritual perspective is generally on being a part of a supportive community, on humility, nonattachment, living virtuously and other practices such as the cultivation of insight, mindfulness and compassionate actions.

It ought to be said that to be classed as a mystic or simply as a spiritually aware person, we need not display or possess any miraculous powers at all, other than the above things mentioned, although technically a true mystic is someone who is seeking to bring his or her life into harmony and profound union with God in some way – of which the above things would be seen as being integral parts of this harmony and unity.

In both Orthodox Christianity and Islam, miracles are not necessarily looked upon as a condition of sainthood, although they are often found in abundance in the biographies of their saints. On the whole Muslim teachings encourage us to look for signs of righteousness, which signify that one is on the right track for living an authentic spiritual life.

As pointed out in this book, Buddhists generally agree that the display of any miraculous power, other than the sixth superknowledge that overcomes all inhibiting patterns, does not always indicate that someone has reached a genuine stage of growth. In his *Autobiography of a Yogi*, Paramahansa Yogananda also stated that, 'Spiritual advancement is not to be measured by one's display of outward powers'. However, we need to be clear here and mention that Yogananda is not referring to powers of compassion or other comparative external acts of spirituality but the exhibition of traditionally understood psychic and miraculous powers and abilities.

In a documentary series called *Transformations* that was made for English television, the English Benedictine monk Father Bede Griffiths mentioned how Roman Catholicism had mistakenly viewed supernormal powers as being either from God or from the devil, whereas in India the distinction between the psychic and the spiritual had been more accurately understood. 'In India', he pointed out, 'they have recognised that there is a vast psychic realm which is neither good nor bad; it is ambivalent'.

I think it is essential to bear Father Bede's observations

79

in mind and realise that it is how the gifts and powers are used and influence our life and conduct that truly determine their worth.

Ultimate Gifts and the Wisdom of Wholeness and Unity

In looking at teachings about psychic, mediumistic and miraculous powers there is a danger in searching for the purely sensational or historical over the ever-present, universal divine consciousness – the God in all that is eternally creating within our Cosmos. The French priest, mystic and palaeontologist Teilhard de Chardin, who was one of the most forward-looking Christians of the last century, was not that concerned with the historical Jesus but in the presence of the evolving Cosmic Christ, the universal divine consciousness that permeates and unites all. As a Christian, Teilhard saw Christ as the creative energy and loving heart of the Cosmos, with the power to unite all things together and animate them into new expressions of community.

The great seers, mystics, and prophets of the past described the powers through the eyes, terminology and understanding of their time. Yet some wisdom and insights of our current age may require us to let a few perspectives and ancient beliefs go, or at the very least to reassess them. Some of the miracles of Jesus for example, where he is reported to have cast out demons, look as though he was in fact helping people suffering from epileptic seizures (Matt. 17:14-15) or psychological disturbances (Matt. 8:28-34).

We know now that many experiences are conditioned by our held beliefs and concepts which can be reinforced by the views of others with whom we share them. Nonetheless, this does not imply that the experiences that unfold on the roads to spirituality will have no value or life-enhancing qualities about them, but merely that they can often draw upon the symbols and beliefs that have some meaning for us, with which we can identify.

The search is always ongoing and calls us to look freshly for answers from the understanding of our current age and invariably requires us to step out of our current thinking in order to discover greater perspectives. We know only too well that traditions can become institutionalised and unhealthily concerned with trying to get everyone to sign up for a set creed or doctrine. Yet generally this is not how they started. With the discovery of the Gnostic Gospels and other important ancient texts at Nag Hammadi in 1945 we have come to see how early Christians were similar to some modern-day seekers and held many beliefs and how spirituality was for them more about a continual and personal quest for truth and transforming oneself.

Yet we will never be in a position where we have all the answers. For that would not only take away the mystics' – of which we have the capacity to be in every moment of our lives as we all have the potential to awaken to oneness with the divine – profound sense of awe and wonder but would bring our evolvement to a complete and uncreative standstill.

I think Bede Griffiths's following observation is worth considering when it comes to the psychic realm, as the point he makes is noticeable at times. His observation reminds us that because of the nature of experiences discovered within the psychic realm that it is a world where unitive states of consciousness and the transforming awareness they bring are not always present:

> *As long as we are in the psychic world it is a world of multiplicity. There are many gods, many angels, many spirits, many powers of various sorts and this is why the psychic world is always somewhat ambiguous.*

What comes over clearest and as the most important in the lives and teachings of various mystics, Buddhas and yogis is the quest for spirituality, instead of religious barriers – compassion and loving one's neighbour being the greatest gifts, and discovering a peace, wisdom and an equanimity that helps us to put our finer qualities to use in practical and beneficial ways. The parable of the good Samaritan demonstrates how compassionate actions are more important than beliefs and rituals and is something we should not forget.

Buddhists place much emphasis on daily life practices. Within Hinduism there is Karma Yoga, which is about making all of our actions skilful and mindful and is perhaps comparable in some ways to the practice of mindfulness in Buddhism. In Islam and Christianity there has often been work done for the poor and sick – charity being one of the Five Pillars of Islam. For the powers themselves, when used by those who have not reflected upon the broader implications of spirituality, can even divide its followers into those who are seen to have the gifts and those who have not, whereas in reality, everyone is endowed with worthy abilities, but it is how we use them that makes them spiritual and profoundly effective. A healthy spirituality values *all* creative abilities and areas of unfoldment and helps them to flourish. For our authentic nature is the key to infinite creative potential that is available for us to use in every moment.

What contemporary science such as Quantum physics and Rupert Sheldrake's theories about morphogenetic fields and resonance are confirming are the insights of some of the great mystics and early indigenous beliefs into the non-separate, interrelatedness of nature and all existence. Such knowledge needs to move us to consider how numerous holistic, integral and spiritual practices can help us touch life more deeply and bring about mutually beneficial enrichment that embraces the needs of all. If the whole is not included in development it can cause a split between the individual and other spheres of life – the spirit world and the physical world are not two separate things – and leave the door open to an unnatural balance of power where those with certain gifts have the final say and cannot be questioned, which discourages free thinking, a spiritually mature acceptance of difference and the wisdom that is within everyone to be truly appreciated and helped to flourish.

It is not that the Spirit, the divine and the realms of spirituality are in the possession of only a certain few as is often seen in unhealthy cults and fundamentalist strands of belief. The ultimate reality is that everyone is in touch with these in an infinite variety of different ways. They are interwoven with and work through all, including ourselves and the Earth of which we are a part. We are after all interconnected with the

Earth and nature. A true guru/teacher in Hinduism will help students to discover the Ultimate Guru, which is universal. For the Hindu philosopher Ramanuja (11th century CE) the whole world was seen as Vishnu's/God's body.

The roads that lead to spirituality are eternally calling us. All we have to do is be responsive and willing to evolve with the Spiritual Universe in which we live. Of which all life is a unique expression. A deep sense of unity with this one in all and all in one can lead us to profound awakenings that exist in every moment and to wholesome actions that healthily participate in life as it unfolds.

Realms of Spiritual Being and Compassionate Actions

We often see various gifts coming to the fore quite naturally when students unfold numerous dimensions of their spiritual nature. An approach that can supply them with the knowledge of how to handle their gifts wisely. To develop any ability without a spiritual basis for good is to be drawn away from the whole of our creative potential and the richer possibilities that can be available to us. In a talk given by Elaine Pagels, she described how people who performed miracles in Jesus's time were pretty much a dime a dozen and speculated that what may have been the reason why Christianity caught on and became so popular was the idea of everyone being equal and included. In a time when most people were living a life of servitude this would of course have been very appealing.

The most important openings lead us to skilful acts of compassion, to wisely and deeply connecting with the unfolding mysteries of life and the Universe, to caring for the Earth and all her inhabitants and biological diversity. For within us there is the creative divine impulse, which is full of wondrous gifts of numerous kinds, not just psychic, shamanistic or mediumistic ones or the traditionally considered miraculous. For just being is miraculous. Rabbi Abraham Heschel reminds us that, 'Just to be is a blessing. Just to live is holy'. But how often are we aware of this miraculousness, this blessing and holiness? How often do we take part in and celebrate the creativity that flows through all and co-operate with the unfolding of it in life?

When there is an awakening to spiritual realms of being it is only natural that every moment and facet of our lives will start to become more harmonious and begin to reach out to deeply embrace and include all (other life, people, faiths and the Earth) in a unifying whole. We have to remember why the Buddha, Muhammad, the Jewish prophets, Jesus and many of the great yogis are remembered. The Buddha in particular, is primarily respected throughout the world for his insights into the human condition, his teachings on nonviolence, loving-kindness, transforming all that inhibits our true nature and how to live in harmony with life and find peace in every step. Without a holistic message of a compassionate unity that transcended religious dogmas and social divisions, Jesus would have soon been forgotten. Muhammad's wisdom, along with his everyday life and conduct are held up as examples for Muslims to live by. The central message of the Qur'an is one of peace and surrender to the spiritual will of the divine – to a life of non-harm and brotherhood and sisterhood with others. 'Let there be no compulsion in religion' the Qur'an states

(2:256). For the majority of Muslims the true message of Islam is about equality, an acceptance of differences and to be a patient, respectful and loving person with no discrimination or unwholesome qualities.

A popular prayer in Judaism calls upon God to establish peace, goodness, blessing, graciousness, kindness and compassion upon us all and upon the people of Israel. The prophetic message of Micah in the Hebrew Bible reminds us that every individual has an obligation to both God and his or her community to act justly, be merciful and walk humbly with God (6:8). Throughout human history, every age has seen those who have distorted such teachings and spiritual examples of being human in order to exclude others for political ends and for self-gain or because of a lack of understanding and ignorance. But the real heroes are those who have lived by teachings of harmony, inclusiveness and unity in diversity, who were invariably inspired at certain times in their lives to call for compassionate action and to speak out when human rights were threatened. In today's world, we also have to consider the rights of non-human species – our more-than-human relations – and include the preservation of nature, of which we are all interrelated. Though us humans often seem to forget this.

On the matter of spiritual inclusiveness I would like the last words to go to the always inspirational and deep ecumenical teacher and activist Matthew Fox from his book *The A.W.E. Project, Reinventing Education, Reinventing the Human*:

From Buddha to Jesus, from Isaiah to Muhammad, from Black Elk to the Vedas of India, from Lao Tzu to the wisdom teachers of Africa, our species is admonished to respond to life with Compassion. Gandhi and Martin Luther King, Jr. are just two who have become 20th century heroes for having done so.

*   *   *

Appendix I

Conversation with Glyn Edwards
on the Powers

Glyn Edwards 1949 – 2015

G lyn Edwards was internationally recognised as one
of the UK's finest mediums and teachers of spiritual
and psychic science. At 16 he joined a Benedictine
community. He later became a protégée of the world-
renowned medium Gordon M Higginson, who was the
president of the Spiritualists' National Union for more than
20 years. Glyn was a regular and highly popular course tutor
at the Arthur Findlay College for over three decades and ran
workshops and demonstrated his mediumship throughout
various continents. He was interviewed on television and

radio, coauthored two development manuals with me and recorded numerous teachings and exercises.

He was particularly known for the quality and depth of his teaching and his ability to demonstrate his mediumship almost effortlessly in front of large audiences. In all the years I knew him, he always read widely and took a deep interest in numerous fields of spirituality, different religious beliefs, various forms of healing and contemporary discoveries in science and psychology. Along with those from Spiritualist backgrounds, students and teachers on his courses could come from a variety of traditions such as Hindu, Christian, Jewish, Yogic, Buddhist, Sufi, Psychotherapist, Reiki Healer and Neo-Pagan, and could be of any age from teenage years to senior citizens.

The following conversations with Glyn took place in my apartment in East London and were especially arranged for them to be included in this book. Interestingly, although he had read an early draft of the book, in some places he raised points about spirituality and areas of development that were parallel to ones I was working on for extra passages, which seemed to show some synchronistic thinking happening between the two of us. In other places, he brought in perspectives that drew deeply on his beliefs and experience as a medium. Questions put to him were invariably followed by a period of reflective silence. He would then answer fluently without pausing until he had covered all he felt was needed to be said.

*   *   *

S: *When did you start to notice that you had the abilities you have? Have they caused you any problems in your development and what has been the spiritual implications of these abilities?*

G: I can remember having experiences that could be classed as mediumistic when I was around four years old. But it was not until I was older and about the age of 18 that I realised the significance of these experiences. In my teenage years I experienced what could be classed as a spiritual crisis, as the experiences were making me take a much broader view of some of the things I had been brought up to believe. And when I started to investigate and be involved in Spiritualistic fields of work I also encountered problems, but of a different kind. As certain abilities unfolded I was given advice that now seems to me to be limiting and does not take into account the spiritual whole of our being. For instance, I was often given the impression that gifts such as mediumship, healing and teaching were abilities that worked separately from one another and if I concentrated on only one area it would not necessarily help with the development of other abilities. Yet as I progressed I found that this was not the case. Like a layer upon layer I discovered that all abilities are interconnected as they are after all parts of our being and link us with the creativity of all life. It is through this that I discovered the need to be open to and realise the oneness and wholeness of spiritual unfoldment.

I realised that any kind of healthy development needed to include and work with many facets of our being, including conflicting parts or any set-backs on the spiritual path in order to unfold an integrative awareness of a sacred wholeness that has the power to bring balance into our lives. From this we realise the true centre of our being that radiates out through all that we do and are. I realised that there could be no limits or boundaries placed on the ultimate essence of our being. For if the divine is limitless and in all, and all is in the divine, then the creative abilities we have must also be limitless.

I have come to see that the spiritual potential within us is not confined. It is we who place restrictions upon it. In my early years I realised that I had to be careful when listening to those who sought to impose rigid beliefs about a separation between different areas of life. What I have now found is that we need to find a sense of freedom within ourselves to face our journey of unfoldment, from which comes a discovery of an inclusive and compassionate understanding that trusts and nurtures the whole of our being. Ultimately, the spirit, the true Self that we are, is deathless, changeless and full of infinite positive potential and seeks harmonious expression through all.

S: The spirit world as mediums and shamans generally think of it is not always there in the same way in other traditions. Can you possibly explain why? Further to this, mediums and shamans often paint a physical and dualistic view of the afterlife that seems rather like life as we already know it, except with a spirit body instead of a physical one. Contemporary science as well as many mystical insights talk more about an interconnected oneness. Where do you stand on this?

G: An interconnected oneness fits more with my own understanding. Beliefs as we know are invariably influenced by the cultures we grow up in and even spiritual experiences are influenced by set beliefs. It is easier for us to grasp aspects of a spiritual dimension if we think of it in similar ways to everyday life. For some it is a helpful way of relating to the spirit world. But we can see that it creates a sense of physicality about it as a means to explain a dimension that is ultimately bound up with and interacting with and through all.

All the great wisdom and mystical traditions have beliefs about an afterlife. Yet all have slightly different perspectives. When it comes to beliefs, I feel we have to consider the point you raised in this book and fleshed out in *The House of Wisdom* about I am right and you are wrong approaches, as they can only lead to divisions and conflicts instead of a respectful acceptance of difference or a mature spirituality that allows us to agree to disagree without being unsettled by another person's opinion. For me and knowledgeable teachers I have felt privileged to have met from numerous disciplines and if we look at what some of the great spiritual teachers of history have had to say about what this other dimension encompasses, we come to realise there are realms where we go beyond concepts and definitions.

I believe just as physical existence is unfolding that the life of a disembodied spirit personality is also evolving toward an interrelated state of pure being and consciousness that is about unity and interconnectedness rather than individual separateness. As to how much my own acquired beliefs have influenced this view, who can say. However, contemporary scientific investigations are starting to confirm much of this understanding, which can be traced back to the insights of various mystical traditions. I do feel however that prevalent beliefs we hold prior to and after death of the physical body can create the image of a physical realm. But from my experience as a medium, this image appears to be quickly dropped as a wider expanse of experience is awakened to.

Other areas of interest are found in the way some spirit communicators describe after death states as being similar to our physical world and yet others do not. We will have to decide for ourselves what is true or not instead of relying on what others tell us to believe.

An individual may undergo spiritual and mediumistic types of experience that seem very real to him or her. Nonetheless, modern psychology warns us that all experiences are invariably coloured by present as well as past systems of belief and previous experience. I think we have to be careful about seeing things as either black or white and accept that there are many grey areas of development before arriving at a clear understanding about some things. This is after all what the word 'development' implies – an ongoing process of evolvement, which includes an evolvement of our beliefs.

Discovering spiritual truths does not always happen overnight. We need to encourage each other and ourselves to work deeply and probe within ourselves and any experiences or openings we have in order to arrive at what is truly valid and ultimately real. For me, one test for contemplating whether something is spiritually valuable or not is if it allows for an inclusion, acceptance and compassionate embracing of others. If it does not, it surely has not gone far enough. For it has not reached that understanding of an interconnected oneness you mentioned.

S: What is your view on grace? Are the powers already there, inherent in everyone, given as a divine blessing as a form of grace, or are they developed?

G: This is a good and important question. However, here we are again entering into realms of belief and it depends on our definition of grace. For me, grace is a sense of giving and receiving which happens not just between the divine and its Creation but is also transmitted from our own human self to others. Ultimate realms of development transcend terms and concepts. Yet at the same time we need them to individually understand certain things about spiritual growth. Grace is a mystical element of unfoldment that is difficult to pin-down to being just one thing. You were telling me recently how in the Jewish faith, life and Creation and its abundance and beauty are seen collectively as a form of God's grace, which is quite a valid view I think.

Grace has within it elements of love, compassion, understanding, wisdom and kindness. It is something that enlarges the mind, our processes of thought, perceptions and awareness and all actions and activities of life. It affects every level of who and what we are and helps us to unfold altruistic and divine qualities in our lives. It can therefore be seen as an important and essential facet of unfoldment, which is sometimes overlooked or not mentioned enough in some spiritual teachings. As to whether psychic, mediumistic or miraculous gifts or abilities are given or developed is something I can only answer from my own understanding.

As far as I can see we are born with a predisposition for these abilities. From my own experience, these abilities take us into realms of potential and therefore into areas of individual possibilities. It is through recognition, receptivity, opening our minds and working with our potential that an awareness of there being no limits to the abilities that we have comes into being. It is we who place limitations and conditions on them. From a supreme perspective it can be seen as the divine within us awakening and opening to itself, so therefore, why would it hold anything back.

Psychic, mediumistic and miraculous powers in this sense are neither given nor developed but are revealed when we remove all that stops us from recognising them as an inherent part of our nature. Development in this area then lies more in how we reach this level of understanding and manifest such powers more purely. For those who wish to explore more about this profound view of spiritual unfoldment, the books by the Christian writer and teacher Joel S Goldsmith are particularly strong on this point of understanding about grace and how God, the divine, is the ultimate power in our unfoldment and in the Universe.

S: In mediumistic trance states there appears to be a loss of consciousness and lucidity. Some reputable mediumistic writers such as Lawrence and Phoebe Bendit, whose books have been published by the Theosophical Society, feel it is not a healthy thing to develop because of this. It also seems to go against some mystical and wisdom traditions' ideas, especially Yoga and Buddhism, about a clarity of mind. What are your views?

G: Here we are entering into an arena that is difficult to fall on any one side. If you look at the teachings of the past and present about trance states and how they can affect a medium, there are various views about them. Some mediums describe a loss of awareness and lucidity experienced in some trance states as actually enhancing their conscious life because another mind separate from theirs has awakened them to something greater than they had originally realised. After being in a mediumistic state of trance, and once the medium has come back to full consciousness and lucidity, the impression left behind in his or her unconscious mind (I use the word 'unconscious' here because in a way the medium has been unconscious to normal surroundings) is described by some to have benefited their life. Some are said to feel healthier, happier and to have a much more expanded view of life because they have opened to another spiritual mind that has blended with them. However, there are others I have known who have talked of a reverse effect.

In certain areas of spirituality, mystics in various traditions describe entering into states of ecstatic awareness in which their consciousness of physical life ceases to exist. Yet areas of psychological research tell us that some yogis who enter into various advanced states of *samadhi* actually experience heightened beta brainwave activities, which are more typically found in intense concentration or even in periods of agitation. Nonetheless, yogis themselves tell us that what they experience is more of an awakened state rather than a loss of consciousness. I think more investigation needs to be done in this area to define what appears to be different types of experience and how they can affect people in different ways. But it seems to me that many mystics are experiencing what can be described as trance-like ecstatic states of awareness.

In the psychology of Yoga and Buddhism, although they both emphasise a clarity of mind, they also promote meditative practices that are bound up with altered states of awareness which can be viewed as forms of entrancement. The practice of *pratyahara* in Yoga, for example, is about the withdrawal of the senses from outward distractions and can be seen as a kind of preliminary trance-like state of awareness. On returning to everyday awareness, mystics from various traditions sometimes described the deep experiences they have as leaving them feeling exhausted, debilitated or challenged in some way. Yet they also describe as mediums have that it heals them, enhances their being and awareness and deepens their spirituality. Some mystics have described how their experiences created an inner conflict between their spiritual and worldly selves. This is an area were modern therapeutic approaches to spiritual development can help in bringing about a balance and harmony between the appearance of different and sometimes opposing parts of our nature and reveal a more congruent, balanced and authentic life.

There are mediums that tell us that the trance states they have undergone, with a loss of conscious awareness, has unfolded what they describe as a clarity of mind that is *perhaps* comparable to what some yogis and Buddhists describe. It is difficult to say one thing or the other. We need to look more closely at what these various states can bring about within the individual without imposing beliefs but decide for ourselves whether the unfoldment of these states is desirable or not for our overall well-being and growth.

We need to be careful before deciding what is useful or not in development as there are clearly realms within realms of awareness where it is hard to draw a clear line and say that this is right and something else is wrong. We must search as widely as we can and decide what is beneficial and right for our unfoldment. There is much food for thought in the Bendit books, and all views can help us to arrive at a spirituality that is more thought-through and life enhancing, but we need to remember that everyone is teaching from their own experience and perspectives and that others may see things differently.

In the mediumistic trance state, there have been those who have entered into it and given evidence of survival after death and various spiritual teachings, yet these have had no effect on their behaviour or changed them for either good or bad. This seems to show that this other world is not here to impose its will upon us but leaves us to decide for ourselves whether to inculcate the teachings and the implications of an eternal spiritual life.

There have been mystics such as Rasputin that evidently had remarkable powers and were able to enter into trance-like states that did not outwardly improve them in any way. I think it is extremely important that we keep an open mind, that we are objective and non-judgemental where trance states are concerned as it is a wide topic and there are many facets to consider.

S: Is there a danger in feeling self-important and somehow separate from others because of the gifts?

G: Yes, of course. We have to be realistic and remember that these abilities do not set us apart from everyday life. If approached from a spiritual perspective they can enable us to engage more healthily with life as it unfolds, rather than standing apart from it. These gifts or abilities, whatever one wishes to call them, can lead us to share in others' joys and suffering instead of thinking that we are in some way more important than others.

If we consider:
- some of the excellent work that has been done by some medical doctors
- the selfless actions of many nurses throughout history
- the kindness of those who have helped build a better world in which to live
- the insights into the heart of spiritual unfoldment some have had, which have become major influences for humanity
- the positive changes social reformers and environmentalists have brought about
- the benefits to human life or the maintaining of a better balance between humankind and nature those leading the way in medical or agricultural research have achieved
- the good work done by those in different fields of educational development
- the healing as well as meaning and purpose that great works of art and music can have

...We see from all these things that mediumistic abilities can help us – if we use them beneficially and inclusively – to see into many realms of spirituality. Such things must surely lead us to a sense of humility and respect for all life and people and to consider all as equal and equally valid for different reasons. We need to understand that every individual and manifestation of life is in fact unique and special, is ultimately sacred, and can have something to offer and enrich our lives.

S: You have studied the lives and teachings of various mystics, lamas, and yogis in depth, such as the Dalai Lama, Ramana Maharshi and various Christian mystics. What has this told you about psychic gifts and spirituality as a whole?

G: That one spills over into the other. That everything can help us to unfold a wider and more inclusive view of spirituality and deeper understanding of ourselves. That what we are is a part of a divine presence that is in and transcends all. Many of the teachings I have looked at have awakened within me an ongoing search to discover and find ways that can best unfold that which is beyond boundaries, to what some might describe as miraculous in some traditions. Additionally, they have brought about a growing awakening to how we are capable of great acts of compassion and kindness and can communicate with and be influenced by realms beyond physical levels of knowing to realising there is an ultimate reality permeating all – described as the *atman*, the soul, the Spirit, the luminous mind, etc. These are merely terms to describe something which is paradoxically immanent and

also transcendent – something that is deathless, sacred and eternal. This takes us beyond the normal seeing, feeling and hearing states of mediumistic and psychic awareness and various miraculous powers to an understanding of there being a profound presence in all that is omniscient and omnipotent, and is continuously creating and evolving.

For the Hindu, the Christian, the Muslim, the Sikh and the people of the Jewish faith, it may be termed as 'God' or 'the divine'. For the Buddhist it will be described as 'Nirvana', beyond descriptions, forms and concepts, as a state of no mind, pure unconditioned awareness, emptiness, neither being nor non-being and as the spiritual core of all – our ever-present Buddha Nature. All of these I believe are interconnected and can lead us to discover realms that are beyond physical existence, which can enable us to touch and commune deeply and profoundly with life, both the seen and unseen, in more wholesome and balanced ways. Development needs to bring about a realisation and understanding of the origin of all things and the unity of life – to live a true state of oneness that recognises that we are not separate from other life and, therefore, spontaneously perform acts of compassion where and whenever possible because of this understanding.

S: What are your views on the general warning made by various wisdom and mystical traditions about psychic and supernatural powers being a possible distraction to spiritual life?

G: On the one hand, seeking mediumistic phenomena may bring about a spiritual transformation in us and a greater capacity to understand the spiritual nature of our being. The difference lies in our individual intentions and aims.

Mediumistic phenomena, whether we are aware of it or not, have at their core the same principles embedded within them as other spiritual practices. On the other hand, I think we can become so immersed in looking just at psychic, miraculous and mediumistic aspects of a tradition that we fail to include other areas of unfoldment. Ultimately such things need to help us realise there is something more to life than just the materialistic realms of existence.

For me, psychic and mediumistic abilities have not only given me an opportunity to communicate with those who have continued their existence after death of the physical body but also to view the cause of all phenomena, to realise that there is that which transcends all and is the Originator, the Preserver and the Creator of all. If we lose sight of this I feel we will be in danger of losing sight of the deeper dimensions of spirituality and any abilities we have will suffer as we will only be going so far with them and placing limitations upon them. If we look at psychic, mediumistic and miraculous powers as the pinnacle of spiritual unfoldment, then it seems to me, and I emphasise *to me* on this point, they would be an obstruction to unfolding other beneficial facets of our nature.

But people need to arrive at their own views about this matter. We have come a long way from times when people imposed rigid beliefs on others and did not allow them the scope to decide and experience for themselves what was right for them and could give their lives deeper meaning, purpose, and direction. We also need to consider some of the points you have raised in this book about how such powers are invariably bound up with a tradition's spiritual path, such as the *siddhis*, which are a part of both the Hindu Yogic and Buddhist paths. Also, I should point out again here about mediums I have known that have displayed and developed their abilities to a great degree, but their abilities did not change them in any way that could be called spiritual. Both sides of the coin need to be considered I feel.

It seems to come down to what we are seeking. If our focus is only on one thing and we are not opening ourselves to other realms of being and awareness, then we are in danger of finding such abilities a distraction to the spiritual whole of unfoldment. It is now recognised that if we develop more than just one type of ability, it enhances others that we have. So we would be limiting mediumistic abilities if we just focus on their development and nothing else. If we are taking a more holistic, integral and inclusive approach we are hardly in any danger of such powers limiting the 'emergence', to use a popular term for development, of our spiritual evolution. When one thinks about it, it's a matter of common sense.

S: What practices have you found helpful for your abilities and how do they affect your daily life?

G: Meditation in the more traditional sense of the word has certainly enhanced my spiritual awareness and its effects have spilled over into enhancing my mediumship. The use of mantra has also affected my psychic and mediumistic awareness. The practice that has come to be known as Sitting in the Power, which was given to me through the trance medium Mark Webb, has particularly aided my abilities and benefited other areas of development because it helps in bringing about an awareness of the Power which is in all. As simple as the practice is I have found that it leads to an awakening to realms of infinite love that integrates the spirit with our world and can be communicated with. This then leads to a realisation that just as human life lives on, so does all life. These practices have enriched my life and enhanced my spiritual search. But it is not over yet, as the search is an eternal one for us all.

Other practices that some might not immediately think of as important parts of development but can help us broaden the abilities we have and take a more holistic approach, involve such things as studying numerous wisdom traditions and spiritual philosophies, which help to open the mind and bring about an understanding and acceptance of those who hold different beliefs about spirituality, and taking in the creative side of life, including music, art, literature, poetry and being amongst nature and cultivating a deep awareness of life's interconnectedness.

I have found that all these things have enhanced my appreciation of and sensitivity towards the creative realms of my own being and the abilities I possess and have intensified a sense of awe and wonder of the divine that is found in nature, of which human nature and creativity is also a part and is the power behind the miracle of Earth-life itself.

S: Do you have practices for mediumistic unfoldment and others for spiritual development? And what advice would you give those who are interested in the development of mediumistic abilities?

G: Within a Spiritualist context the answer is yes. I have over the years sat in a circle with others and even by myself for mediumistic development so that the link to the spirit world may build a stronger bond. I am sure different teachers in this field will have their own views about how different areas of development interlink or can be awakened to. However, I would like to deal with the practice of attunement with the spirit from the perspective of a medium's awareness. To sit in the stillness and the quietness and invite the spirit world to work with and through us I think is important, as the invitation we extend shows a willingness to co-operate with the spirit and what may unfold through this. Through inviting the spirit to blend with our consciousness and make itself known through our senses, mediumistic abilities can in my experience be brought into being. At first there needs to be this intention of being willing to co-operate, eventually followed by letting this intention and willingness go, allowing our thoughts to become calmer and more settled and adopting an attitude of receptivity to different levels of being.

I think it is important that a developing medium comes to *truly know* who is working with him or her in the spirit world. By knowing I do not necessarily mean by name or nationality, but learning through the communication that is established, the identity of those working with him or her and begin to recognise how the development of mediumistic abilities influences a medium and how communication shapes itself through his or her individual awareness.

Today there are some who are only interested in quick-fix approaches. There have always been aspects of spiritual, psychic and mediumistic development that can be cultivated quickly. But no matter what field of unfoldment we are looking at, to come to a stage of deeply knowing how different areas of growth work and relate to numerous levels of being takes time and dedication. It is only through this dedication and deeper knowledge that a true and lasting development is established. Unfortunately, some do not wish to study and work deeply with their abilities and see how they can be expanded, how mediumship functions, how contact with different spirit personalities can shape perceptions and awareness, how spiritual insights can surface and the unfoldment of various gifts can enrich our lives.

Another area for consideration is to do with choice and how to integrate the things that open to us as we move forward, such as a fuller understanding of the spiritual principles and implications behind the communication and how these can widen our perceptions of life and influence our everyday conduct.

If we apply these things we will be able to manifest the potential we have more fully. Practices such as Sitting in the Power that I mentioned before, which help us to expand our mind and consciousness to realms of the seen and unseen, enable us to know for ourselves that the power within us can touch the power that is in everything. And the more we do this adds to our unfoldment and can bring us to a state of oneness and unity with all.

There is a tremendous amount of data available to us about people who have undertaken certain practices within their own faith and wisdom traditions that brought about different states through prayer, Yogic and Buddhist meditation, mantra and so on, who have experienced other levels of reality and realms of communication. Through such practices, phenomena have manifested of both a mental and physical kind. It is not just through what some may term as 'mediumistic practices' that such things have occurred.

An illustration of what I mean by this can be seen in some of Swami Dharmananda Saraswati's Hatha Yoga students, who experienced spontaneous awakenings to clairvoyant, clairaudient and clairsentient abilities, which were totally unsought and came about because of the Yogic practices they were doing. It is partly because Swamiji experienced this herself that she investigated some aspects of Spiritualistic phenomena in order to gain a better understanding of what was unfolding in her own development.

We need to realise that status, nationality, spiritual backgrounds or beliefs have nothing to do with the phenomena of mediumship. The abilities are a natural part of our being. Except our beliefs will invariably colour our perceptions about them. Because these abilities work through our finite physical mind, our prevalent state of mind and the concepts we possess will condition their manifestation. This is one reason why we need to include other practices such as those based on spiritual principles and understanding as they can help us to transcend limiting concepts, beliefs and the world of finite thought, and can open us to the Infinite Mind that is present in all. And so help us to grasp more of what the ultimate truth of life and eternal existence implies.

Practices that can be found in mediumistic unfoldment can be called practices of intention and attention. By applying these two principles to a yearning to know the mysteries of continuous life and the truth of our spiritual being, they can bring about profound awakenings to who we really are, why we are here and where we are going on our spiritual journeys, and an embodiment our authentic nature.

S: Sometimes we hear of healers and mediums giving advice that does not seem helpful. Sometimes with little concern for the consequences of their actions. There are also times when their information is incorrect. What are your views on these things? How are people meant to approach the advice or information they are given?

G: These are important questions and ones that need to be looked at openly and frankly so that we can work towards a mature and practical spirituality that acknowledges possible problems and looks for areas for improvement. Inaccurate information that may sometimes be given by mediums or healers can lie within their own perceptions and not working enough with their abilities to arrive at a true state of knowing. They might judge things at the time as being correct. But we also have to take into consideration that from one perspective we have a human side to our nature that is not without its limitations and restrictions and can at times affect the quality of mediumistic work. Communicators in the other world tell us they are also undergoing stages in their evolution, which seems to indicate they do not necessarily have all the answers and may well be seeing things from perspectives that are not without limitations either.

I think we need to be sensible and realise that our beliefs about, as well as the actions we take in life, are our responsibility. We must reflect upon things that we are told in mediumistic sittings and decide for ourselves what is helpful or not, just as we would with advice given to us in regular life. Like any ability, there is always room for improvement. Mediumship is by no means a perfect science. Some that communicate with us through mediumship, though their intentions are good, there are times when there are problems in the transmission of the information given. This is why it is important for a medium in all stages of his or her development to be vigilant as to the validity of any information given to him or her. We ought to inform sitters about any evidence or information or advise transmitted to them during a sitting that to the best of our knowledge we feel what is being said is correct. But sitters should be prepared to accept only that which can be proven as factual.

I think it is essential to realise that the two levels of communication that exist within mediumship are an evolving experience between the medium who is learning how best to apprehend information coming from the spirit world and this other level of reality learning how best to transmit information to the medium. Every sitting and message is really an experiment with no guarantees. All we can do is see what unfolds and decide for ourselves what is helpful or not.

A particular problem area is our conscious physical mind's perceptions, as we are working with an imperfect instrument – even though the human mind is possibly the most complex mechanism, if we can call it this, in the Universe. But perhaps this is why it can at times cause problems. Interestingly, all the great wisdom and mystical traditions touch upon teachings about blindness of our true consciousness, so therefore, our unfoldment needs to be about realising the limitations of our finite mind and discovering ways in which it can be better utilised and made a purer and more receptive instrument for the dissemination of truths.

The mediumistic journey is in many ways multifaceted and needs to be open to evolvement at all times. Yet because of the nature of evolvement, it means there will be times when new ways of working unfold, of which we will be unfamiliar. I remember you shared some experiences in the first book we wrote together about how you were once subjectively aware of some images that could at first be interpreted in a certain way, as they actually appeared, but they needed to be probed to arrive at their true meaning as they were in fact symbolic representations of people's surnames. If information was given as first perceived, it would not have been accurate. It shows how we have to work with mediumistic impressions instead of being quick to say what we are first perceiving to be true. We therefore need to check any impression or information received for its validity and consider how best to transmit it to those that would be the recipients of it. This I feel is why mediums need to include honesty and integrity in their development, as I believe these will affect the fruits of their work.

S: On the one hand some people might think being in touch with spirit people a bit strange. On the other hand, these same people might consider being in touch with divinity as more of a natural experience. What would you say to such people?

G: We cannot separate the spirit world from the divine as everything is interrelated. If as I believe all life survives and is interconnected, then why should it appear strange to commune and be in contact with different realms of existence? In all the great wisdom and mystical traditions this contact with other realms has been mentioned and has at various times throughout history to the present day been practised. In some traditions, people who walked this Earth have come to be revered as saints, gods or goddesses and there are accounts of communication with these people in nonphysical after death states.

We also need to consider how throughout the ages ancestor worship has been intrinsically bound up with many traditions even to this day, how there are accounts about those that have been described as angelic beings communicating with various people, and how some have prayed to different individuals such as saints, as they are seen as intercessors before God who will act on people's behalf. There are also shamans and oracles who are consulted in various traditions and many renowned mystics have displayed mediumistic types of abilities.

It seems to me that there has always existed in humankind's psyche the belief in nonphysical realms of existence. Early indigenous people and shamans were the first humans to connect with a spirit world permeating nature and to communicate with their departed ancestors. Others have looked towards the more transcendent areas of spirituality. Although there are some who have never completely separated themselves from some of the early indigenous beliefs and practices, there are some who have, which has led to an unhealthy separation between nature and the spirit. All areas need to be included in the search for the one ultimate reality that expresses itself in and through all.

If we accept that life is eternal and there are other realms of existence intertwined with our physical world, then it must surely be a natural step in our evolution to be able to communicate with these other realms and with those who are living on. We need to recognise that there are different ways in which to approach the many faceted dimensions of spirituality and be open to numerous areas that can lead us to healthier states of spiritual being and embrace the all-ness of what eternal life is about.

* * *

Appendix II

Conversation with Glyn Edwards on Spirituality

Santoshan (Stephen Wollaston) and Glyn Edwards. Taken in 1989.

S: *Who has particularly impressed you and why?*

G: Ramana Maharshi is one of many. His central teaching was based around the age-old question 'Who am I?' which obviously leads to self-inquiry and can help us put aside any doctrines or distractions that inhibit our unfoldment. Out of asking himself this simple question there arose a natural goodness within him that embraced all people, irrespective of their individual beliefs, theories or backgrounds. I have also been drawn to the ideals and life of Mahatma Gandhi, who sought a peaceful settlement without violence, as well the Dalai Lama, who has trod a similar path. These two spiritual giants have endeavoured to live by the principles of their beliefs and have in many ways changed the world in which we live. Showing us by example, ways that we can truly be and the power of individual and collective nonviolent action, which highlights a central tenet of spirituality. They have both showed us that the only solution to all the conflicts of human nature is to love and care compassionately for one another – a core teaching that goes back to Jesus, the Hebrew Bible, the Buddha and many influential yogis and spiritual teachings.

There are numerous other people and writers that have inspired me such as MP Pandit – who we were both fortunate enough to meet in India – and Aurobindo for their practical and integral approaches to development, and Earnest Holmes for his profound commonsense about spirituality.

S: You have just touched on the next question, which is what do you see as the most important thing or things on spiritual paths and can you give reasons for why you think it or they are important?

G: As well as what has been said, other facets of importance are about having determination, dedication and a mind that is receptive to the creative and wholesome possibilities of what can unfold in our life.

Although others may touch our lives and guide us, we are responsible for our individual unfoldment. As we enter into development with an open mind and a willingness to grow into spiritual maturity, which means including the inevitable difficulties and suffering we and others encounter, along with blissful moments of awakening to divinity, we begin to realise that all life is ultimately One – that there is no clear division between set systems of belief or everyday life and spiritual understanding. Behind all there is that which is creative, the same Spirit in all, which has imbued all life with the ability to express its creativity, to become co-creators, and has allowed humanity to discover life's true purpose and meaning – that ultimately everything is ruled by love and that our true nature is ultimately loving.

S: In life there are often various crossroads to face and it can be difficult at times to know the right path or action to take. Is there any advice someone who is highly intuitive like yourself can give about this?

G: Deep intuitive wisdom that can guide us in the right actions in life takes time and patience to develop and requires us to cultivate various powers such as reflective reasoning, knowledge based on experience and an acceptance of things as they really are. Life is always about moving on and evolving in the eternity of existence and each of us needs to face each moment, each passing phase of life with wisdom, acceptance and compassionate understanding. We are all imbued with intuitive abilities, but we need wisdom and compassion as well in order to be able to reflect upon and learn from various situations encountered in life and find paths on which our actions can benefit not only ourselves but also others.

There is no point in living with regrets if things have not

turned out as we feel they should, as the past has gone and the only thing that can be changed about it is how we respond to and are influenced by it in the present. There also needs to be an awareness of and a creative responsiveness to what new events and undiscovered potential may unfold. We are infinite and because we are infinite we obviously have no beginning or end. Our beginning-less and endless Self does not need to view life as missed opportunities but seeks to call us to ways in which we can skilfully manifest our true nature, our divine attributes, more purely in every moment.

S: Some have ideas about spiritual people being very placid and taking life's problems lying down. Yet we find people such as Matthew Fox, who has been one of the most influential teachers around over the last few decades, mentioning in his autobiography how he sent a seventy-page document to someone who underhandedly tried to stop his ordination being accepted, even though the person was unsuccessful anyway, and people such as William Wilberforce, Martin Luther King Jr and Mahatma Gandhi hardly seemed inactive when it came to matters of injustice and inequality. What are your views?

G: The part of us that believes in justice needs to express itself. Some Christians even go as far to condone what they see as righteous anger, which is different to an immature, self-centred childish anger that arises because we cannot have our own way.

Spirituality embraces actions that can bring about positive changes where and whenever possible. To think of the divine and spiritual development as purely transcendent and to overlook the immanent, omnipresent, feminine and creative aspects of its sacredness has arguably led us to our current state of destroying the Earth and not caring enough about a balanced life, injustice, inequality and poverty. I know that this is something you have also taught and have touched upon in your book with Swami Dharmananda.

It seems to me to be about the age-old quest for finding a balance between doing and being – a development of an awareness of things as they are and states of equanimity, along with an affirmation of life rather than an escape from it. Although suffering exists and physical life is transient and forever undergoing change, it does not mean that we should not take part and find meaning and purpose in life – even at the risk of displaying our human qualities. Life on Mother Earth is not a negative place that we feel we would be only too pleased to escape. Her beauty inspires awe and wonder and has great healing qualities.

Yes, there have always been those who have retreated from life and there are many arguments for and against this. But to make an ideal about spiritual people being placid leaves out much of what spirituality is about. We find the Buddha choosing a middle path and many notable mystics in charge of monasteries and/or religious communities, such as Hildegard of Bingen and Teresa of Avila, which when you read about their lives you see their positions required them to make difficult choices and sometimes take a definite stand for what they saw as fair and just.

If we study the lives and biographies of some of the great masters of spirituality, those that have brought about great changes or have profoundly influenced people's lives, no matter how advanced we might consider them to be, we ought to never lose sight of the fact that they still had human qualities. ('Keep me away from the wisdom which does not cry, the philosophy which does not laugh', the mystical poet Kahlil Gibran said.) Invariably, they are not people who could be described as placid but have been people of action, social change and profound teachings. It is their sense of humanity and human justice that often spurred them on to do great things and impart exceptional wisdom. Some have even displayed outbursts of anger about injustice that has driven them to bring about positive changes in the world, and others have possessed what might be described as all too human weaknesses. But in spite of such weaknesses, it does not undermine the work they have done. It shows us how the spiritual path is not always easy. I noticed in one of Matthew Fox's books on one of the most important Christian thinkers in history, Thomas Aquinas [see *Sheer Joy: Conversations with Thomas Aquinas on Creation Spirituality*], that he wrote about him having clay feet and saw nothing wrong with that.

Our human nature and character is bound up with our individual personality, which does not necessarily imply being unhealthily ego-centred as some mistakenly believe. Ego and personality are different things of course, as we can have a healthy spiritual-centred personality just as much as an unhealthy ego-centred one, of which there are numerous important realms of unfoldment between the two.

Sometimes we think of spirituality in terms of idealistic

routes of expression that do not allow for the complexities of existence and different facets of a person's life. There is often a problem of placing people we admire on pedestals as we invariably become disheartened when they do not live up to the unfair projections we place on them, which probably no one could live up to.

We can also beat ourselves up when we do not live up to unrealistic ideals we impose on ourselves. There are often reasons why we act less than we feel we should. This is why great teachers such as Jesus taught that we should not judge lest we be judged [Matt. 7:1]. 'Never judge someone until you have walked a thousand miles in his or her shoes' as the Chinese saying goes.

Let us allow others to be as they are and follow their own paths of evolution, physically, emotionally, mentally, morally and spiritually. Although I believe that at an ultimate level of reality we are not human beings unfolding to spiritual experience but spiritual beings experiencing human realms of existence [Glyn referring to and paraphrasing a popular saying that is often accredited to Teilhard de Chardin]. To me, this points to something that is within human experience which is evolving through the activity of a spiritual force within us and in all life in the Universe. It indicates, as previously mentioned, that development is about learning how to overcome all sense of separation from our true nature.

We should never lose sight of the fact that the Spirit within all is constantly seeking to refine the finite and to express itself more purely through all. This is why unfoldment, awareness, compassion and wisdom are key areas of spirituality, as they lead us to purer states of being, knowing and acting in everyday life.

S: People sometimes take the stand that spirituality is not about traditional wisdom and study but about their own experiences. What do you think about this?

G: I can understand why some might feel the need to reject traditional religious ideas and want to discard any investigation into them, as there are areas that need to be re-evaluated and made more relevant to our current age. But we have to be careful of throwing the baby out with the bathwater. To rely purely on individual experience without other areas of development can make it hard for us to know how to apply, embody and integrate experiences, as well as have the language to even talk about and understand them and, therefore, share our experiences with others. I remember you telling me about some of the work you had done in schools, where some children as young as 11 responded positively to learning new terms and language which enabled them to then talk openly about spiritual experiences they had had. As adults we can have resistance to learning new things, but if we truly wish to grow we need to overcome our resistances and explore the real issues behind them.

However, to follow a path of purely intellectual study without some personal insight and experience is also not the best route. It needs to be a balance of the two – the heart and mind in fact. There is much in our unfoldment that requires some points of reference. To ignore the writings and teachings of both the past and present is to ignore the evolution of our spiritual brothers and sisters and the insights they have had about spiritual unfoldment. We will obviously have to be discerning with what we study. This too is an important practice and a part of the process of unfoldment.

There is of course a need to base our moving forward on our experiences, but there is also a need to constantly reflect upon how our experiences are affecting our beliefs and overall growth into an authentic Selfhood that embraces all. It is clear that on one level religious experiences can separate and divide people into different camps where they feel they have the only truth and that others have somehow got it wrong. This is why it is important to study, widen our understanding, find common ground, honour others' beliefs and realise that we are all in our own individual way searching for that which ultimately unites us – a supreme non-separate truth and sacred reality.

There is also the fact that no one person can know everything and there have been those in various traditions that have looked at different areas of spirituality that are essential and can help us, and from which we can draw much food for thought such as matters concerning modern ethical dilemmas, political and social change, physical and psychological benefits of various practices and so on.

We must embrace the Light that shines through other faiths, other ways of thinking and traditions. An open mind to others is essential. If we are considering spirituality from a mediumistic perspective, we ought to consider what the spirit world is ultimately about. Is it not all-encompassingly bound up with all traditions, life, creativity, evolution and people, and most importantly with those trying to help humanity realise its spiritual nature and compassionate potential?

Combining insights and teachings of the past and present along with personal experience, can spur us on to discover deeper and more valid universal truths, with the hope that what we find, embody, live out and share will benefit others we walk with on our paths.

S: Finally, although much of what you have said could be seen to cover this question, can you summarise what spirituality means to you as it can mean different things to different people. On the one hand, some teachers and writers think of spiritual realms of development as being about mystical union or deep states of meditation. On the other hand, if we are using the word to describe anyone who has a natural sense of goodness about them and about wholesome unfoldment and actions in daily life, we are obviously using the word in a much broader way.

G: Yes, it can be used to mean different things. For me it is about an embracing of all people, life and nature, to truly see and value the good in all traditions and in different forms of wisdom. It is bound up with realising that the same supreme Spirit exists in all – that the activity of the psychic, mediumistic and miraculous and the phenomena which come from these, must never restrict the potential for spiritual awareness and a recognition of equality or restrict practices of kindness, natural goodness and compassionate actions.

How can we judge that a carpenter or stonemason may

not just through his or her work develop profound spiritual qualities, and from this have great influence on others who know him or her and his or her work? Additionally, are cathedrals and temples not built by such people whose names we rarely know? Who are we to say that an agnostic is not a spiritual person? Or are we seeking to impose a set system of belief that excludes certain people because they do not hold the same views and practices as we do?

Let us realise that spirituality is more than just meditation practices, rituals, beliefs and personal experiences. It encompasses the all-ness of life. Neither is it a truth that only a few possess or a philosophy which makes us stand coldly separate from life.

Because some have gifts such as insight into other worlds that are seen to connect with ours or have the ability to heal, we should not believe these things set them apart from others or indicate they are more advanced or important than anyone else. Everyone has within them the potential for the same divine qualities, which can be brought to the surface at any point in their lives. Sometimes we may be unaware that we are entertaining angels, meaning anyone who displays natural goodness, as the New Testament passage reminds us, and is one of many reasons why we need to consider showing kindness to strangers [Heb. 13:2], such as when someone listens to our troubles and truly empathises with us. Is this not as valid a spiritual act as any that we can think of? True and spontaneous selfless acts of kindness and compassion are really the core of spirituality.

It is time that all of us, no matter what tradition or none, took a step back and reviewed what is meant by 'spirituality'. Although mediumistic awareness can be seen as a natural part of our being, just as breathing and kindness are, it is only a facet of the whole. Let us apply the principles that we may term as 'higher living'. This is not about seeing ourselves as more advanced than others or separate or aloof from everyday life but manifesting our greatest gifts and recognising there is goodness in all people, including ourselves, even though our human nature can get in the way of displaying it at times as the symbol of *ying* and *yang* reminds us with the white spot in the black and the black in the white – reminding us that no person is entirely perfect, as equally as there is no one who is entirely bad.

We need to cultivate an understanding and a state of being that accepts and loves others and ourselves and realise that our true nature is endeavouring to help us to awaken to the reality of what spirituality is and how to live deeply and skilfully by it in every moment. In looking into ourselves for the greatest gifts we possess we discover the gifts of wisdom and Self-knowledge that are the gateways to freedom, true peace and enlightenment. Such things help us to find unity in diversity and the compassionate Spirit in all.

S: Thank you Glyn for being so open and sharing your thoughts, feelings and personal experiences over these two sessions.

*   *   *

Glossary

After Death States – various wisdom and mystical traditions mention having knowledge of different realms of existence encountered after death of the physical body.

Allah – the Islamic word for God.

Apports – objects that are materialised with the aid of a physical medium and the spirit world.

Astral – a non-physical psychic realm where the physical body is sometimes said to have a double (an astral body). In Hinduism, the astral and subtle realms are interchangeable terms.

Astral Projection – the ability to expand one's awareness to non-physical realms of consciousness. Some believe in an astral body having the ability to travel to other realms and places. The idea of astral projection has been around for thousands of years and can be found in ancient Chinese beliefs.

Atman (Self) – the eternal true Self in Hindu spirituality that can be seen as individual (*jivatman*: innermost being), universal and transcendent, connecting with the ultimate ground of all (see *Brahman*).

Attunement – the ability to blend/attune one's awareness with psychic, spiritual or mediumistic states of consciousness. It functions in numerous ways, such as how we relate to nature, with all life and the many aspects of the divine within us and in all things.

Aura – different levels of energy surrounding the physical body which are connected with numerous facets of one's being: the physical, emotional, mental, spiritual, etc.

Authentic/True Nature or Self – the part of our being that is divine and connects with all. It can be viewed as having an individual, universal and ultimate transcendent facet to it, which has the power to harmonise conflicting parts into a synthesised and sacred whole and help us to find unity with all. Modern psychology also uses these terms but will not necessarily relate them with the divine. Branches of Buddhism use the term 'Buddha Nature' instead of authentic or true Self.

Bhakti Yoga (path of devotion/love) – a devotional path towards the divine or towards a teacher as a manifestation of the divine.

Bilocation – an ability to appear in two places at the same time.

Brahman – in Hindu spirituality it is the one ultimate reality within (*apara-Brahman*) and beyond (*para-Brahman*) the many forms of the Universe.

Buddha (one who is awake) – someone who is enlightened and has woken up to the truth and is seeing things clearly and as they really are. It also refers to the historical Buddha.

Buddha Nature – there are two aspects to it: developable and naturally abiding within us. It transcends thought, is thoroughly pure, undefiled, empty of all dualities and experienced as a joyous expansiveness with infinite positive potential.

Chakra (wheel) – a principal energy centre in the psychic/subtle body.

Channelling – a term sometimes used to describe spiritual teachings given through a medium while in a trance-like state.

Chi – in Daoism it is a vital energy and life force.

Clairaudience / Clairsentience / Clairvoyance – The ability to see (clairvoyance), hear (clairaudience) or feel (clairsentience) the divine, discarnate spirit personalities or things of a psychic nature, either subjectively or objectively, has existed in all the great wisdom and mystical traditions, and indigenous and tribal traditions throughout the ages. They have been viewed by many great masters as being natural abilities that can be awakened through spiritual practices such as meditation, contemplative prayer and yoga exercises, whether one is consciously trying to develop them or not. In Yoga traditions they are referred to as the *siddhis*. The Buddha taught about developing the divine ear and the divine eye and seeing into past lives and the reasons why people suffer and are reborn. Clairaudient, clairsentient and clairvoyant abilities are found in Christian mysticism and have been displayed by numerous saints. The word 'clairvoyance' is sometimes employed to refer to mediumistic abilities in a general way by the media and in the public arena.

Collective Unconscious – an underlying interconnected consciousness that is a part of nature and life. Carl Jung believed it housed powerful archetypes and memories which can be traced back to the beginnings of human thought.

Consciousness – to have a level of self-awareness. In spiritual traditions consciousness is not seen to rely on just the physical body for its existence and is often viewed as functioning in numerous ways, such as on an individual and universal level, as well as in ultimate transcendent states of mystical experience.

Contemplation – can simply refer to reflecting on life and one's experiences. In Christian mysticism it is a form of prayer that is comparable to Yogic and Buddhist forms of meditation.

Cosmic Intelligence or Cosmic/Universal Consciousness – a creative interconnected mind that came into being with the Creation of the Universe, of which we are all a unique part and can be realised in transcendent states of consciousness.

Creation-Centred Spirituality – a spirituality which looks for ways to become co-creators with the divine and find harmony with the creativity of the Earth and Universe. Its roots can be found in the Christian mystical tradition and in Tantra, connected with various *chakras* and with Shakti (the creative divine Mother energy), and with aspects of Sufi, Buddhist, Daoist, ancient Celtic, African, Australian Aboriginal, Native American and Hasidic Jewish spirituality. The visionary priest, theologian and activist Matthew Fox has done much to promote the teachings of Creation Spirituality over the last few decades, of which four paths/ways are mentioned: 1. The *Via Positiva*:

the way of awe, delight and amazement; 2. The *Via Negativa*: the way of uncertainty, darkness, suffering and letting go; 3. The *Via Creativa*: the way of birthing, creativity and passion; and 4. The *Via Transformativa*: the way of justice, healing and celebration.

Dark Night of the Soul – a period of spiritual dryness that is seldom lit by any uplifting spiritual experience. Nonetheless, it is invariably seen as a stage of progression and purification on the mystical path, where restrictions of the individual 'I' are overcome.

Development Circle – a gathering of people who meet in order to develop spiritual, mediumistic and psychic gifts and abilities. The origins could possibly be traced back to indigenous practices of sitting in a sacred space represented by a circle and the saying of Jesus about two or three people gathering in his name.

Dhikr – a word used by Sufis meaning 'remembrance' and refers to the practice of remembering God often.

Direct Voice Phenomena – refers to a form of physical mediumship where the voice of a discarnate spirit personality is made physically audible.

Divine – an ultimate sacred interconnectedness which works and is universally present within our Cosmos and also transcends it.

Dukkha (unsatisfactoriness) – one of three marks of existence in Buddhism. It is often translated as 'suffering' into English, but the word 'unsatisfactoriness' is now seen as a more accurate translation.

Earth-Centred/Gaia-Centred/Nature-Centred – concerned with environmental and global issues, and seeing oneself as an interconnected part of the Earth and Earth as a living organism.

Ecozoic Age – a phase of the Earth's history requiring humans to live at one with the Earth's needs and finding mutually beneficial enrichment.

Ectoplasm – a substance that is said to be a mixture of physical and non-physical material used in physical mediumistic phenomena by the spirit world in order to materialise individual spirit personalities and physical objects (apports). Other traditions may have connections with this area, such as some of the phenomena witnessed around the lives of various saints. However, further investigation is still needed.

Ecumenism and Deep Ecumenism – ecumenism was originally a movement within Christian spirituality seeking to unite different Christian churches and denominations, which has since been widened by some to also be about seeking unity amongst different world religions, which is sometimes called 'deep ecumenism' to distinguish it from being solely about Christian churches and denominations.

Ego – a wide term that can mean different things to different people. In mystical and Eastern wisdom it refers to our individual sense of self, to self-centredness and how we see ourselves as separate from other life.

Engaged Spirituality – a spirituality that seeks to bring about beneficial changes in society and the world.

Enlightenment – a state of being where one has woken up to seeing and embodying the ultimate truth, though different traditions and branches of faith have various views about it.

Etheric Energy – comparable with *prana* and *chi* energy, and seen as a vital energy working in and surrounding the body and as a universal life-force.

Fana – a word used by Sufis meaning 'passing away', and refers to dying to the world and finding survival in God.

Gaia Theory – seeing Earth as a living organism. A theory put forward by the influential environmental scientist James Lovelock.

Global Spirituality – spirituality concerned with global issues.

Grace – a blessing and/or gift from God that helps a seeker move forward in his or her evolvement. Life and Creation itself are also seen as gifts from God and, therefore, part of God's grace in traditions such as Christianity and Judaism and some devotional schools of Hinduism. Arguably, the concept of grace is not in the historical Buddha's teachings, whereas later in different strands of Mahayana Buddhism a form of grace that helps spiritual seekers starts to come in.

Guides/Spirit Guides – discarnate spirit personalities that are believed to interact with the physical world and aid people's development.

Guides/Spiritual Guides – people who help others in their spiritual growth such as a guru in the Yogic tradition.

Guru (teacher) – in Indian traditions it can refer either to a spiritual teacher who dispels ignorance and suffering or to the divine/God as the supreme guru.

Hatha Yoga (yoga of force) – a branch of yoga that places emphasis on physical postures, cleansing techniques and breathing exercises.

Healer – someone who heals with the interaction of the spirit world, or through the use of prayer or affirmations, or anyone who can restore someone to a state of well-being through a variety of methods, such as naturopathic remedies, holistic practices, acupuncture or the laying-on of hands at an Evangelical meeting.

Higher Self – a part of us which houses our finest attributes and qualities such as compassion, kindness and wisdom.

Holiness – a state of being near to God. Being holy or made whole.

Holism – a theory about matter, nature and the Universe interacting and being made of living organic wholes – that all life and things are more than the sum of their parts.

Holistic – including and harmonising the whole self: the body, feelings, emotions, mind and spiritual levels of being.

'I'/the 'I' – the individual self that we see as separate from other people and things, which has associations with the ego (self-centredness). It should be noted that Western psychology has many different theories about the ego.

'I'/the True 'I' Consciousness – the ultimate Self/reality (a non-separate state of consciousness).

Illumination – mystical visions, experiences and openings of the mind and consciousness.

Immanent – when used to refer to God, it refers to God as being ever-present.

Integral Spirituality – a spirituality that includes many traditions, disciplines, insights and practices of both the East and West such as contemporary cosmology, ecology and psychology and Eastern philosophy and practices, and looks for an integration of the whole of our individual, social and universal selves.

Integral Yoga – a synthesised path of self-discovery and expression formulated by Sri Aurobindo: a unitive path of perfection, bhakti (devotion), jnana (insight and knowledge) and karma (action) yoga, which aims for a spiritual purification and transformation of the complete personality.

Interconnectedness (non-separateness) – that everything shares an interrelationship.

Interfaith – seeking for an open dialogue and an acceptance of difference and finding of common ground between different religions.

Interspirituality – a contemporary term coined by the lay monk Wayne Teasdale. Refers to an integration and dialogue of people following different spiritual practices and beliefs. It is for those seeking to overcome barriers between different faiths and incorporate practices and insights from different spiritual traditions.

Intuition – the ability to know information without the aid of the physical senses. In spiritual literature intuition is often associated with wisdom and profound levels of insight, but it can function in everyday levels of knowing about something being right or wrong and in everyday hunches.

Intuitive – an alternative word for someone who is mediumistic and/or psychic. It has many links with intuition (see above).

Jnana Yoga (yoga of knowledge) – Yogic path to freedom via wisdom, discernment and intuitive insight.

Kabbalah – a mystical branch of the Jewish wisdom tradition.

Karma (action) – refers to 'actions having consequences' and the will, which have an effect on one's spiritual progress, in either a positive or negative way, in this life or a future one.

Karma Yoga (yoga of action) – a path that leads to spiritual liberation through skilful willed actions.

Kundalini Yoga (yoga of psychic energy) – a path that seeks liberation through the use of creative psychic energy.

Liberation – freedom from psychological states and worldly conditioning that restrict the true spiritual nature of our being.

Lower Self – part of our being that is in disharmony with its true spiritual nature, and has connections with the shadow part of ourselves.

Mandala (circle) – circular design representing the Universe and a particular deity.

Mantra Yoga – the repetition of mantras as a path to liberation. Words, sounds or short affirmations are repeated in order to affirm an aspect of the divine, which is often represented by the name of a specific deity. In Mahayana Buddhism mantras are often used for bringing about an awakening to spiritual qualities within oneself and insights into the ultimate nature of existence.

Maya – can have many meanings, such as the ultimate creative power in the Universe or the world of 'illusion' or 'delusion' in Hindu spirituality. It can also be interpreted as 'misconceptions'.

Meditation – can imply many different types of practices. In Christian spirituality meditation can refer to visualisation and more reflective practices. In Yogic traditions it can be about focusing one's attention on an object, on the breath or on a mantra. The contemporary Christian Meditation Movement, founded by the English Benedictine monk John Main promoted Yogic forms of meditation such as mantra and various breathing exercises.

Mediumship – the ability to see, hear or feel spirit personalities that no longer have a physical existence. Additionally, trance and physical mediumship and healers who are aided by spirit personalities are other areas that fall under this heading. The word literally refers to someone who is in the middle of two realms of existence and acts as a mediator between the two.

Mind/Higher Mind – a wide term which has connections with the discriminating faculty and the rational mind (the intellect) as well as wisdom and insight.

Mind/Lower Mind – automatic unconscious functions of the mind.

Mind/Unconscious Mind (individual unconscious) – levels of the mind that we are not consciously aware of, which include instinctual drives and memories of all past experiences that can affect our personality on a conscious level. The spiritual, psychic and psychological implications of an unconscious mind are vast, as it cannot only be seen to link with parts of ourselves that carry subliminal influences that affect our conduct but also with the collective unconscious mind that links with all things in the Universe.

Moksha (liberation) – freedom from conditioned worldly existence.

Monism – the belief in there ultimately being only one reality behind the many forms of life and matter in the Universe (both seen and unseen).

Morphogenetic Fields and Resonance – a biological field permeating nature which contains information to shape the exact form of living things as well as its behaviour. Cambridge biologist Rupert Sheldrake is particularly known for this theory. It has comparisons with Carl Jung's theory of the Collective Unconscious. It has many psychic and spiritual implications concerning an interconnected creative and psychic mind working within nature.

Mudra (seal) – a hand or whole-body gesture used in meditation. It includes invoking an opening of awareness while doing the *mudra*, such as realising one's spiritual nature or the joining of individual consciousness with omnipresent and transcendent divine consciousness.

Mystic – a person who seeks through meditation or contemplative prayer to attain unity with the divine.

Mystical Experience – a wide variety of experiences are often placed under this heading, but a true mystical experience would imply having an experience of union or oneness with God.

Mysticism – a life of prayer and/or meditation, work and discipline dedicated to serving and finding unity with God.

Myths – myths or legends about heroic struggles or personal sacrifice can be seen as powerful archetypes – as symbolic metaphors for the spiritual journey. Joseph Campbell found many myths that were common to all wisdom traditions, which tell important stories about the spiritual seeker's individual search for truth and his or her return home.

Near-Death Experiences – spiritual, religious and out-of-body experiences people have had when they have almost died.

Nirvana – a state of enlightenment achieved in meditation practices.

Nonattachment – it is essential to understand that nonattachment is not about being aloof and separate from life, just as we would not consider the cure of an illness as being about taking medicine that merely numbs our feelings and physical senses and makes us unaware of any pain. Nonattachment encompasses acknowledgment of and being unbound by any restrictive feeling or mental state.

Non-dualism (non-separateness) – the belief that while all things appear to have an individual uniqueness, everything interconnects with an underlying unity (see Monism).

Omnipotent – all-powerful.

Omnipresence – everywhere and in everything.

Omniscient – all-knowing.

Oneness – a state of being in harmony with all things.

Out-of-Body Experience – an experience where one's consciousness seems to leave the physical body.

Pantheism – the belief in a divinity that is present in all things.

Panentheism – the belief in a divinity that is present in all things in the Universe and beyond. An omnipresent and transcendent divinity: God in all things and all things in God.

Perennial Wisdom – a belief that underlying all the great wisdom traditions there is a universal truth running through them.

Physical Phenomena – an area of mediumship which deals with how the spirit world can bring about materialisations of spirit personalities, dematerialise physical objects and rematerialise them again, or recreate the audible voice of a spirit personality.

Pluralism – theologically implies there being more than one principle at work in the Universe.

Pranayama – the practice of overcoming limitations of the body and mind through the use of *pranic*/psychic energy, particularly with the aid of breathing exercises.

Prayer – there are many forms of prayer. For example, some Christian practices of contemplative prayer are comparable to Eastern practices of meditation. Other forms of prayer can include affirmations, reflecting on sacred texts (termed *lectio divina* in Latin) or asking for divine help (petitionary prayer).

Projection – negative parts of our character and personality that are denied and projected onto others.

Psyche – the inner instrument through which we think, feel and discriminate. It consists of the lower, higher and unconscious mind and our individual sense of self.

Psychic – someone who has the ability to know things without the aid of the physical senses, or something that cannot be explained by accepted laws of science. The word also refers to psychological levels of being and levels connected with the unconscious mind.

Psychic Abilities – different traditions have called psychic abilities by different names such as the *siddhis* in Hinduism, in which the ultimate *siddhi* is the realisation of one's true nature and liberation from restrictive states of existence.

Psychometry – the ability to psychically feel into physical objects and obtain information connected with the object.

Quantum Theory – an area of science that studies the laws of physics that are happening on a very small scale. Of particular interest in this field is the discovery that on a sub-atomic level there is no clear separation between people, objects and other phenomena – that there is an ultimate interconnectedness between all.

Qur'an – the holy book of the Islamic tradition.

Reincarnation – the belief that after death the soul or spirit is physically reborn, or unextinguished fuels (anger, ignorance and desire) cause our individual consciousness to be reborn into other realms such as the physical realm, the heavenly realm, the realm of hungry ghosts or fighting demons, as mentioned in the Buddhist tradition. However, it should be noted that these realms can be interpreted as different psychological states of being that we slip in and out of numerous times a day.

Sacred – that which embodies the truth of a religion or an aspect of divinity and is, therefore, something to be in awe of as well as revered, respected and cherished because of its preciousness. To see all as sacred and holy.

Saint – another word for a holy person; someone who is seen as virtuous and lives or lived in the divine's presence.

Samadhi – the climax of Yogic meditation practices where one realises the true Self.

Samsara – the world of conditioned existence in the physical world, which is tied up with ideas about the continual cycle of lives: birth, death and rebirth. It is seen as a world of unsatisfactoriness that we reinforce individually and collectively with our minds and beliefs, which do not show us how things really are.

Samskaras – unconscious imprints and impressions left by voluntary acts which affect our psychological self (see Karma).

Seer – someone who has visions of a prophetic nature and/or can perceive things beyond physical realms of existence.

Self-awareness – to be conscious of one's inner feelings, thoughts, emotions, desires, motives, exterior actions and one's true Self.

Self-realisation – to realise one's full potential and/or one's relationship with the divine.

Shadow/the Shadow – the parts of ourselves that we do not accept and are often hard for us to own.

Shakti (power/force) – the ultimate reality in its creative and female aspect, which acts in the Universe. It is also connected with Kundalini Yoga.

Shaman – someone who has the ability to contact and enter into the spirit world.

Skilfulness – the ability to be spiritually creative in everyday life and conduct ourselves in a manner that brings about balanced living.

Soul – a wide term that can mean different things to different people. For some it is looked upon as the same as the individual spark of the spirit in all; for others it can be associated more with the psychological self.

Spirit – can have different meanings such as one's individual spirit or used as a plural to refer to those who no longer have physical existence. It can also be used as another word for the divine and the sacredness of all.

Spirit World – can refer to an interconnected reality that permeates all, a spiritual existence, or a world that is inhabited by individual spirit personalities.

Subconscious – sometimes used as an alternative word for the unconscious mind (although the latter is generally seen as larger, deeper and not as easy to be aware of as the subconscious), or to describe thoughts, feelings and actions that are just beneath surface levels of awareness, which can be accessed by the conscious mind, and was termed the 'preconscious' by Sigmund Freud.

Subtle Body – a psychic body mentioned in different traditions that can include the *chakras* and different elements (earth, fire, water, air and ether) and energies, as well as emotional and mental realms.

Sufism – the main mystical branch of Islam.

Superconsciousness – has associations with different states, such as hearing astral sounds, seeing visions and experiencing cosmic energy which can lead to a realisation of the divine's omnipresent and transcendent nature. Such things can be seen as being higher and lower levels of superconsciousness, all of which can lead to an opening to one's authentic spiritual nature.

Surrender (letting go and letting God) – the practice of letting go of the individual will and handing one's thoughts, ideas and actions over to the divine or to more spiritual states of consciousness.

Synchronicity – random events that take on symbolic meaning such as a bird flying into a room signifying bad news or natural coincidental events that are seen as miraculous happenings.

Tantra (continuity) – refers to Tantra Yoga and its teachings, which focus on the use of *shakti* energy.

Tapas (heat) – refers to austerity, which may be done for the purpose of overcoming the body and purifying oneself. The word was also used to refer to psychic powers in early Yogic teachings.

Torah – a wide term that includes God's law as revealed to Moses.

Trance – a wide term which can refer to deep mystical states where one is not aware of the exterior world or to different types of mediumistic phenomena where a spirit personality can control a medium's or Spiritualist healer's consciousness and actions. But it should be noted that there are different and subtle degrees in which this is said to happen. For example, a medium might be entranced by a spirit personality but still be aware of and influence aspects of what is being said and happening.

Transcendent – levels beyond normal physical experience.

Transfiguration – to be transformed into a pure spiritual state of being. In Christianity it also refers to the account of Jesus appearing in radiant glory to three of his disciples. As a Spiritualistic phenomenon it is associated with changes brought about in a medium's facial appearance in order to take on physical characteristics of a discarnate spirit personality.

Transpersonal – states of consciousness beyond the boundaries of personal identity.

Unfoldment – a similar word to development which refers more to the removal of things that stop us from recognising and manifesting our true spiritual nature. Unfolding authentic qualities and wisdom and working towards a spiritual synthesis that influences the whole of our lives.

Unitive Consciousness – in Christian mysticism it is where the ultimate mystery is realised and the seeker recognises his or her co-relationship with the Creator. A non-separate consciousness.

Visionary – in spiritual traditions it can refer to someone who has prophetic gifts or teaches profound wisdom about the future.

Yahweh – Hebrew word for God.

Yantra (device) – a geometric design that represents one's individual self and a particular deity. It is used for meditation purposes and realising one's ultimate nature.

Yoga (to yoke/to bind together and become aware of unity with the divine) – in Hindu traditions the most popular forms are bhakti (yoga of devotion/love of the divine), karma (yoga of actions/works), and jnana (yoga of wisdom/discerning intuitive insights). Yoga is also practised in the Buddhist and Jain traditions.

*   *   *

Bibliography

Abhayananda, S, *Mysticism and Science: A Call for Reconciliation*, O Books, Winchester and New York, 2007.

Affifi, AE, *The Mystical Philosophy of Mhyid Din-Ibnul 'Arabi*, SH Muhammad Ashraf, Lahore, 1979.

Arberry, Arthur J (translator), *The Koran*, Oxford University Press, Oxford, 1983 (reprint).

— , *Sufism: An Account of the Mystics of Islam*, Unwin Paperbacks, London, 1979.

Aurobindo, Sri, *Record of Yoga: Volume 2*, Sri Aurobindo Ashram Publication Department, Pondicherry, 2001.

— , and the Mother, *The Psychic Being: Soul: Its Nature, Mission and Evolution*, Sri Aurobindo Ashram, Pondicherry, 2003 (reprint).

— , *The Yoga of Sleep and Dreams: The Night-School of Sadhana* (compiled with an introduction by AS Dalal), Sri Aurobindo Ashram, Pondicherry, 2004.

Baldick, Julian, *Mystical Islam: An Introduction to Sufism*, IB Tauris and Co. Ltd, London, 1992 (reprint).

Benson, Herbert, *Mind/Body Interaction – including Tibetan Studies*, chapter three in *Mind Science: An East-West Dialogue* (edited by Daniel Goleman and Robert Thurman), Wisdom, Boston, 1991.

Berry, Thomas, *Evening Thoughts: Reflecting on Earth as Sacred Community* (edited by Mary Evelyn Tucker), Sierra Book Club, San Francisco, 2006.

Bodhi, Bhikkhu, *In the Buddha's Words: An Anthology of Discourses from the Pali Canon*, Wisdom Books, Boston, 2005.

Bourgeault, Cynthia, *The Wisdom Jesus: Transforming Heart and Mind – a New Perspective on Christ and His Message*, Shambhala, Boston and London, 2008.

Bowker, John, *The Complete Bible Handbook*, Dorling Kindersley, London, 1998.

— (edited by), *The Oxford Dictionary of World Religions*, Oxford University Press, Oxford and New York, 1997.

Brockington, JL, *The Sacred Thread*, Edinburgh University Press, Edinburgh, 1996 (2nd edition).

Carty, Rev Charles Mortimer, *Padre Pio: The Stigmatist*, Tan, Rockford, Illinois, 1973.

Chilton, Bruce, in *Voices of Gnosticism* (interviews by Miguel Connor), Bardic Press, Dublin, 2011 (eBook edition).

Chopra, Deepak, Foreword in *The Visionary Window: A Quantum Physicist's Guide to Enlightenment* by Amit Goswami, Quest Books, Wheaton, Illinois and Chennai, 2000.

Christie-Murray, David, *Voices from the Gods: Speaking in Tongues*, Routledge and Kegan Paul, London and Henley, 1978.

Davies, Stevan, in *Voices of Gnosticism* (interviews by Miguel Connor), Bardic Press, Dublin, 2011 (eBook edition).

Dharmananda, K Sri, in the introduction to *The Dhammapada* (translated with an introduction by K Sri Dharmananda), Sasana Adhiwurdi Wardhana Society, Kuala Lumper, 1992 (2nd edition).

Dowman, Keith, *Masters of Mahamudra: Songs and Histories of the Eighty-Four Buddhist Siddhas*, State University of New York Press, Albany, 1985.

— , *The Sacred Life of Tibet*, Thorsons, London, 1997.

Ebert, John David, *Twilight of the Clockwork Gods: Conversations on Science and Spirituality at the End of an Age*, Council Oak, Tula and San Francisco, 1999.

Eliade, Mircea, *Yoga: Immortality and Freedom*, Princeton University Press, New Jersey, 1990 (reprint).

Ehrman, Bart D, *How Jesus Became God: The Exaltation of a Jewish*

Preacher from Galilee, HarperOne, New York, 2014 (eBook edition).

— , *Jesus, Interrupted: Revealing the Hidden Contradictions in the Bible (and why we don't know about them)*, HarperCollins, New York, 2009 (eBook edition).

— , in *Voices of Gnosticism* (interviews by Miguel Connor), Bardic Press, Dublin, 2011 (eBook edition).

Evans-Wentz, WY (editor), *The Tibetan Book of the Dead*, Oxford University Press, Oxford, 1960 (reprint).

Farges, Albert, *Mystical Phenomena: Compared with their Human and Diabolical Counterfeits*, Burns Oates and Washbourne, London, 1926.

Feuerstein, Georg, *The Yoga-Sutras of Patanjali*, Inner Traditions International, Vermont, 1989 (reprint).

Fischer-Schreiber, Ingrid, Ehrhard, Franz-Karl, Friedrichs, Kurt, and Diener, Michael S, *The Rider Encyclopedia of Eastern Philosophy and Religion*, Rider, London, 1989.

Fox, Matthew, *The A.W.E. Project: Reinventing Education, Reinventing the Human*, CopperHouse, Kelowna, BC, 2006.

— , *Creation Spirituality: Liberating Gifts for the People of the Earth*, HarperSanFrancisco, San Francisco and New York,1991.

— , *Original Blessing: A Primer in Creation Spirituality*, Tarcher/Putnam, New York, 2000 (reprint).

Frankel, Estelle, *The Wisdom of Not Knowing: Discovering a Life of Wonder by Embracing Uncertainty*, Shambhala, Boulder, 2017.

Frazer, Sir James, *The Golden Bough: A Study in Magic and Religion*, Wordsworth, Hertfordshire, 1993 (new edition).

Gombrich, Richard F, *How Buddhism Began: The Conditioned Genesis of the Early Teachings*, Athlone, London and Atlantic Highland, New Jersey, 1996.

Goring, Rosemary (editor), *Chambers' Dictionary of Beliefs and Religions*, BCA, London, New York, Sydney, Toronto, 1992.

Govinda, Lama Anagarika, *Foundations of Tibetan Mysticism*, Rider, London, 1983 (reprint).

Griffiths, Bede, *The One Light: Bede Griffiths' Principal Writings* (edited with a commentary by Bruno Barnhart), Templegate, Springfield, Illinois, 2001.

Guiley, Rosemary Ellen, *Harper's Encyclopedia of Mystical and Paranormal Experience*, Castle Books, Edison, New Jersey, 1991.

Gunaratana, Mahathera Henepola, *The Jhanas in Theravada Buddhist Meditation*, Buddhist Publication Society, Kandy, 1988.

Hecker, Hellmuth, *Mahamoggallana: Master of Psychic Power*, chapter two in *Great Disciples of the Buddha*, by Nyanaponika and Hellmuth Hecker (edited by Bhikkhu Bodhi), Wisdom, Boston, 1997.

Jacobs, Alan (translated by), *The Gnostic Gospels: Including the Gospel of Thomas and the Gospel of Mary Magdalene*, Watkins Publishing, London, 2006.

John of the Cross, St (translated by Kieran Kavanaugh and Otilio Rodriguez), *The Collected Works of Saint John of the Cross*, ICS, Washington, DC, 1991 (2nd revised edition).

Jung, CG, *Jung on the East* (edited and introduction by JJ Clark), Routledge, London, 1995.

— , *Memories, Dreams, Reflections*, Fontana Press, London, 1995 (reprint).

King, Karen L, *The Gospel of Mary Magdala: Jesus and the First Woman Apostle*, Polebridge Press, California, 2003.

— , in *Voices of Gnosticism* (interviews by Miguel Connor), Bardic Press, Dublin, 2011 (eBook edition).

King, Ursula, *Spirit of Fire: The Life and Vision of Teilhard de Chardin*, Orbis Books, New York, 1996 (5th reprint).

Knight, Michael Muhammad, *Muhammad: Forty Introductions*, Soft Skull, New York, 2019.

Krishna, Gopi, *Higher Consciousness: The Evolutionary Thrust of Kundalini*, Julian Press, New York, 1994.

Lerner, Michael, *Spirit Matters*, Walsch Books, Boston, 2000.

McKnight, Scot, *The Jesus Creed: Loving God, Loving Others* (with a foreword by John Ortberg), Paraclete Press, Brewster, Massachusetts,

2005 (4th reprint).

Malcolm, James F, *Psychic Influences in World Religion*, Spiritualists' National Union, Stansted, 1966.

Manser, Martin (compiled by), *Bible Quotation Collection*, Lion Publishing, Oxford, 1999.

Mabry, John R, *The Way of Thomas: Nine Insights for Enlightened Living from the Secret Sayings of Jesus*, O Books, Winchester and New York, 2007.

Meyer, Marvin (translated with an introduction by), *The Gospel of Thomas: The Hidden Saying of Jesus* (with an interpretation by Harold Bloom), HarperSanFrancisco, New York, 1992.

— (edited by), *The Nag Hammadi Scriptures: The International Edition* (with an introduction by Elaine H Pagels), HarperSanFrancisco, New York, 2007.

Nanamoli, Bhikkhu, *The Path of Purification: Visuddhimagga*, Buddhist Publication Society, Kandy, 1991.

Nanasampanno, Acariya Maha Boowa, *Venerable Acariya Mun Bhuridatta Thera: A Spiritual Biography*, A Forest Dhamma Publication, Udorn Thani, 2003.

Nasr, Seyyed Hossein, *Sufism and the Integration of the Inner and Outer Life of Man*, Temenos Academy, London 1999.

Pagels, Elaine, *Beyond Belief: The Secret Gospel of Thomas*, Pan Books, London, Basingstoke and Oxford, 2005 (3rd reprint).

Prabhavananda, Swami, and Isherwood, Christopher, *How to Know God: The Yoga Aphorisms of Patanjali*, Vedanta Press, California, 1981 (reprint).

Primack, Joel, and Abrams, Nancy Ellen, *The View from the Centre of the Universe: Discovering our Extraordinary Place in the Cosmos*, Fourth Estate, London, 2006.

Rahula, Walpola, *What the Buddha Taught*, Gordon Fraser, Bedford, 1967 (2nd and enlarged edition).

Rama, Swami, *Living with the Himalayan Masters*, Himalayan Institute, Honesdale, 1978 (revised edition).

Redfield, James, *The Celestine Prophecy: An Adventure*, Warner Books, New York, 1994.

Robinson, James M, *The Gospel of Jesus: A Historical Search for the Original Good News*, HarperSanFrancisco, New York, 2006.

Rukmani, TS, *Siddhis in the Bhagavata Purana and in the Yogasutras of Patanjali: A Comparison*, chapter sixteen in *Researches in Indian and Buddhist Philosophy: Essays in Honour of Prof Alex Wayman* (edited by Ram Karan Sharma), Motilal Banarsidass, Delhi, 1993.

Santoshan, *The Miraculous Self*, appendix two in *The House of Wisdom: Yoga Spirituality of the East and West*, by Swami Dharmananda and Santoshan, Mantra Books, Winchester and New York, 2007.

Schimmel, Annemarie, *Mystical Dimensions of Islam*, The University of North Carolina Press, Chapel Hill, 1978 (3rd edition).

Schmidt, Roger, *Exploring Religion*, Wadsworth, Belmont, California, 1988 (2nd edition).

Schucman, Helen, *A Course in Miracles: Text, Workbook for Students and Manual for Teachers*, Foundation for Inner Peace, Hill Valley, California, 1992 (2nd edition).

Skorupski, Tadeusz, *The Religions of Tibet*, chapter twelve in *The World's Religions: The Religions of Asia* (edited by Friedhelm Hardy), Routledge, London, 1990 (reprint).

Spong, John Shelby, *Born of a Woman: A Bishop Rethinks the Virgin Birth and the Treatment of Women by a Male-Dominated Church*, HarperOne, San Francisco, 2009 (reprint).

Staal, Frits, *Exploring Mysticism: A Methodological Approach*, University of California Press, California, 1975.

Teresa, St, *The Life of Saint Teresa by Herself*, Penguin, London, 1959.

Thittila, Maha Thera U, *The Fundamental Principles of Theravada Buddhism*, chapter 2 in *The Path of the Buddha: Buddhism interpreted by Buddhists* (edited by Kenneth Morgan), Motilal Banarsidass, Delhi, 1993 (reprint).

Thurston, Herbert SJ (edited by JH Crehan), *The Physical Phenomena of Mysticism*, Burns Oates, London, 1952.

Underhill, Evelyn, *Mysticism: A Study in the Nature and Development in Man's Spiritual Consciousness*, Methuen and Co. Ltd, London, 1930 (12th revised edition).

Vogl, Adalbert Albert, *Therese Neumann: Mystic and Stigmatist, 1898-1962*, Tan Books, Rockford, Illinois, 1987.

Waida, Manabu, *Miracles*, article in *The Encyclopedia of Religion: Vol. 9* (edited by Mircea Eliade), Macmillan, New York and London, 1987.

Wilber, Ken, *The Essential Ken Wilber: An Introductory Reader*, Shambhala Publications, Massachusetts, 1998.

Wilson, Bryan, and Dobbelaere, Karel, *A Time to Chant: The Soka Gakkai Buddhists in Britain*, Oxford University Press, Oxford, 1994.

Woods, James Haughton, *The Yoga-System of Patanjali: Or the Ancient Hindu Doctrine of Concentration of Mind*, Motilal Banarsidass, Delhi, 1992 (reprint).

Yogananda, Paramahansa, *Autobiography of a Yogi*, Self-Realization Fellowship, California, 1993 (12th reprint).

Main Bible Reference

The HarperCollins Study Bible: Fully Revised and Updated – New Revised Standard Version (Harold W Attridge, general editor of revised edition; Wayne A Meeks, general editor of original edition), HarperOne, San Francisco, 2006.

Audio Reference

Elaine Pagels, *The Gospel of Thomas: New Perspectives on Jesus' Message*, Sounds True, 2006.

Internet References (October 2007 and *July 2018)

www.allexperts.com/q/Hindus-946/Miracles-Krishna.htm

www.catholicnewsagency.com/news/mary-magdalene-apostle-to-the-apostles-gets-upgraded-feast-day-77857*

www.iqra.net/Hadith/miracle.php

www.menorah.org/starofdavid.html

www.mohammad-pbuh.com/3/othermiracles.htm

www.parami.org/buddhistanswers/what_about_miracles.htm

https://sunnahonline.com/library/history-of-islam/281-miracles-of-the-prophet-muhammad-the

www.ted.com/talks/susan_david_the_gift_and_power_of_emotional_courage?*

https://en.wikipedia.org/wiki/A_Course_in_Miracles

https://en.wikipedia.org/wiki/Bible_prophecy

https://en.wikipedia.org/wiki/Muhammad#Seal_of_the_prophets

*   *   *

About the Author

Stephen Wollaston was given the name **Santoshan** (contentment) by an English swami and is a OneSpirit Interfaith Foundation minister. He holds a degree in religious studies and a postgraduate certificate in religious education from King's College London. He also trained in psychosynthesis counselling and typographic design. In the late 70s he was the principal bass guitarist of one of London's first punk rock bands, The Wasps.

He has taught world religions and other humanities subjects, English language and academic writing at various educational establishments in the UK and at a medical university in the Middle East. He is a Council member of GreenSpirit, the main typographic designer of GreenSpirit magazine and the GreenSpirit Book Series, and an author, coauthor and editor of over a dozen books, including *Spirituality Unveiled: Awakening to Creative Life* and *River of Green Wisdom: Exploring Christian and Yogic Earth Centred Spirituality*.

He was a close friend of the UK medium and former Benedictine monk Glyn Edwards for 26 years, coauthored two books with him and edited an anthology of his teachings.

*   *   *

Reflections with Glyn Edwards, More Reflections, and the Complete Collection

Compiled and with Additional Material by Santoshan (Stephen Wollaston)

The *Reflections with Glyn Edwards* anthologies are full of wonderful quotations by Glyn for meditation and reflective purposes, and include additional passages by Glyn's long-time close friend Santoshan (Stephen Wollaston) from the books they worked on together and individually.

Mid-price paperbacks
142, 137 & 252 pages
ISBN 978-1080308798
ISBN 979-8397188913
ISBN 798860848986

Low-cost eBook editions available from Amazon and Smashwords. Hardback editions also available.

'His insight into and experience of an array of interrelated realms of spirituality was unquestionably phenomenal and deeply profound.'
~ From the compiler's introduction

Glyn Edwards
A Renowned Medium Remembered
~ Collection of Memories and Teachings
Compiled by Santoshan (Stephen Wollaston)

A unique collection of Glyn's inclusive wisdom on spiritual and mediumistic realms of unfoldment as well as a wonderful tribute book that honours his life and work. In this combined treasury of Glyn's teachings and memories about him, numerous insights and fond recollections are shared alongside various photographs. It includes a detailed biography about him, heartfelt stories by people whose lives he touched, and a collection of quotations, articles, workshop sections and exercises by Glyn, which give practical steps for awakening to the ever-present world of the spirit and the oneness of spiritual living.

112 pages
ISBN : 978-0-9569210-4-8

eBook edition available from Amazon and Smashwords. Hardback edition also available.

'Many people are not aware how outstanding a medium and teacher Glyn in fact was… There are no adequate words to express the void that has been left without his physical presence.'
~ Ron Jordan (Devadūta), internationally renowned medium and spiritual teacher

Rivers of Green Wisdom
Exploring Christian and Yogic
Earth-Centred Spirituality
Santoshan (Stephen Wollaston)

In *Rivers of Green Wisdom* the author shares personal reflections on Christian, Yogic and Earth-centred wisdom and key stages encountered on his own spiritual journey. The book unveils central teachings about the sacredness of Earth and Nature, covers both past and present understanding about our interdependent relationship with the natural world, and how various teachers have looked for East-West fusions for deeper and more responsible living.

86 pages
ISBN 978-0-9935983-2-6

*Low-cost paperback
and eBook*

'Seldom do you find such practised clarity in revealing the wisdom of Spirit.'
~ Sky McCain, Vedantist and author of
Planet as Self: An Earthen Spirituality

Pathways of green Wisdom
Discovering Earth-Centred Teachings in
Spiritual and Religious Traditions
Edited by Santoshan (Stephen Wollaston)

Pathways of Green Wisdom covers teachings and practices that promote honouring and compassionately caring for Nature. It brings together numerous reflective and informative pieces by contributors to GreenSpirit magazine spanning a period of 11 years, along with especially written new material. Contributors include progressive and insightful writers from different backgrounds. Each offers an enriching well to draw some nourishment and appreciate numerous Earth centred dimensions of a particular spiritual path.

140 pages
ISBN 978-0-9935983-3-3

*Low-cost paperback
and eBook*

*The above two books are
part of the GreenSpirit
Book Series. For more
details visit
www.greenspirit.org.uk*

'This is a wonderful book, which takes you on a journey through various traditions.'
~ Ian Mowll, interfaith minister
and the coordinator of GreenSpirit

148 pages
ISBN 978-1978414716

*Low-cost paperback
and eBook*

Dark Nights of the Green Soul
From Darkness to New Horizons (expanded edition)
Edited by Ian Mowll and
Santoshan (Stephen Wollaston)

The book highlights insights about facing difficult times, alongside reflections on our interactive relationship with Nature and present various perspectives about working with darkness and ways in which to creatively move forward. It includes personal stories and explains how each of the storytellers found new meaning and growth by either connecting with an animal friend or in Gaia-centred spiritual awakenings and teachings. The book also reflects upon the state of our planet and offers practical views for the times in which we live and 'the great work' we need to embrace.

'*Dark Nights of the Green Soul* is a compact, intelligent and highly accessible addition to the GreenSpirit Book Series.'
~ Chris Holmes, GreenSpirit council member

152 pages
ISBN 978-1986435017

*Low-cost paperback
and eBook*

*The above two books are part of the GreenSpirit Book Series. For more details visit
www.greenspirit.org.uk*

Awakening to Earth-Centred Consciousness
Selection from GreenSpirit Magazine
Edited by Ian Mowll and Santoshan
(Stephen Wollaston)

Awakening to Earth-Centred Consciousness shares personal stories, engages thoughtfully with green topics, and provides insightful teachings about our interrelationships with the natural world. It encourages us to embrace an inclusive, compassionate and mindful spirituality – one that leads to interacting with deep levels of life and Nature, of which we are all wondrously interwoven and a part, and the essential obligations this brings for responsible Gaia-centred living.

'A delightful book to dip into for GreenSpirit's existing supporters and a good way to get a feel for GreenSpirit for people who are new to the organisation.'
~ Jane Stott, GreenSpirit council member

144 pages
ISBN 978-1-84694-509-0

*Low-cost eBook edition
(shown above) available
from Amazon and
Smashwords*

Spirituality Unveiled
Awakening to Creative Life
Santoshan (Stephen Wollaston)
Foreword by Ian Mowll

A succinct and compelling synthesis of numerous
spiritual traditions. Whilst weaving together insights
from contemporary and past masters of spirituality,
along with holistic and Earth centred wisdom, it
beautifully highlights teachings about the essentials
of creative unfoldment. Invites readers to join in
the important search to find a healthy interaction
with life. Key areas include the power of creativity,
the effects of positive and negative actions, and
harmonious living with the natural world.

**'Integral thinking at its best … a masterful
synthesis … '**
~ Marian Van Eyk McCain, editor of
GreenSpirit: Path to a New Consciousness

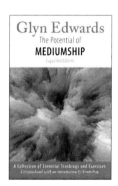

128 page expanded
edition
ISBN 978-0-9569210-3-1

*eBook edition available
from Amazon and
Smashwords. Hardback
edition also available.*

The Potential of Mediumship
A Collection of Essential Teachings and Exercises
(expanded edition)
Glyn Edwards
Compiled and with an introduction by Santoshan
(Stephen Wollaston)

The Potential of Mediumship presents an inspiring
collection of teachings, along with numerous
essential exercises for unfolding mediumistic and
spiritual gifts. In this first ever anthology of Glyn
Edwards's wisdom, he shared first-hand accounts
about his own mediumistic experiences and
imparted profound insights that will help you to
move forward with your abilities. There are chapters
here for beginners and the more advanced that
reveal how the spirit world can communicate with
and work through us and prove survival of life after
death.

'There should be many more books like this!'
~ Psychic News

160 pages
ISBN 78-0-9569210-0-0

eBook edition available from Amazon and Smashwords. Hardback edition also available.

The Spirit World in Plain English
Mediumistic and Spiritual Unfoldment
Glyn Edwards and Santoshan (Stephen Wollaston)
Foreword by Don Hills

The Spirit World in Plain English is a revised and updated edition of the authors' first book. In this beneficial manual, Glyn Edwards and Santoshan share practical exercises and teachings for discovering inherent mediumistic and spiritual potential. Together, they combine their knowledge in far-reaching ways and cover numerous essentials for understanding and interacting with the ever-present world of the spirit.

'This book is more than just another book on spiritual and psychic development; it's literally the bible on development.'
~ Amazon UK (customer review of 1st edition)

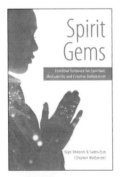

128 pages
ISBN 978-0-9569210-1-7

eBook edition available from Amazon and Smashwords. Hardback edition also available.

Spirit Gems
Essential Guidance for Spiritual, Mediumistic and Creative Unfoldment
Glyn Edwards and Santoshan (Stephen Wollaston)

Spirit Gems is a revised and expanded edition of the authors' second book, which provides practical steps for discovering how to live more freely, deeply and peacefully. Glyn Edwards and Santoshan write beautifully whilst covering essentials such as living in the now, facing our fears, finding unity with all and harmonising the whole of ourselves. Both authors share profound insights for immersing our lives in spiritually and mediumistically centred living. Their down-to-earth wisdom weaves skilfully through various levels of individual unfoldment and enriching realms of transforming experience.

'A must for anyone's bookshelf.'
~ The Greater World Newsletter (review of 1st edition)

From Punk Rock to Green Spirituality
Santoshan (Stephen Wollaston)

A collection of eleven articles by the author, which include Caring for Our Sacred Earth, Awakening to Creative Life, Celebrating Our Interconnectedness with Nature, A Postmodern and Age-old Wisdom of the Heart, and Expanding Our Circle of Awareness.

Low-cost in all formats
104 pages
ISBN 9798511082547

The House of Wisdom
Yoga Spirituality of the East and West
Swami Dharmananda and Santoshan
(Stephen Wollaston)
Foreword by Glyn Edwards

The House of Wisdom covers starting out and challenges on the spiritual path, and the Yogic understanding of our authentic Self.

'A real treasure-house of spiritual knowledge.'
~ Julie Friedeberger, author of
The Healing Power of Yoga.

224 pages
ISBN 978-1-846940-24-8

GreenSpirit Reflections
Compiled by Santoshan (Stephen Wollaston)

A meditations book of profound and inspiring quotations on green spirituality. Drawing from a variety of GreenSpirit publications, this little book of relections gathers together numerous key insights in nine essential categories that can be seen as the core of Earth-centred wisdom.

118 pages
ISBN 978-1-846940-24-8
*Low-cost paperback
and eBook*

CDs and books by Glyn Edwards available from Mind-Body-Spirit Online:
Website: www.mindbodyspiritonline.co.uk
Tel: (01202) 267684 (outside UK: +441202 267684)

Downloads of recordings by Glyn Edwards available from:
www.listening2spirit.com